INFOCUS

How to Stop Side Hustling & Make One Business Pop

ROBERT L. PRICE

CONTENTS

FOREWORD

H aving more than one thing that you're good at is both a blessing and a curse. On the one hand, you are a jack of all trades, but, on the other, you're a master of none. In my experience, those who fit this bill have outstanding intentions and can talk a good game but, last time I checked, intentions and jaw-jacking don't pay bills. Narrowing that field of skills and fully investing in the gift you were designed to perfect is the name of the game.

That narrowing is called focusing, and; there's no better book I've read that speaks to this process than Infocus. There's nothing wrong with a side hustle. When done right, that "hustle" can provide a stable secondary stream of income. But, when they're all you have going for you, you're burning the candle at both ends and in an unsustainable position. If you want to lock in on your calling with laser focus and make that one true calling and business "pop," then Infocus is the book for you.

Dr. Eric Thomas, Founder, Eric Thomas & Associates, LLC

INTRODUCTION

I f you are anything like me, your problem might not be that you can't find what you are talented at. Your problem might be the curse of having too many things you're good at, and feeling confused about which you should commit to.

This may start you down a long road of endless side hustles because of your many talents. In my case, I did countless businesses such as multi-level marketing, apparel, music, film, training and development, mini-golf, spiritual development, sports analysis, and finally, real estate.

As an optimist, I never started a business endeavor or movement that I didn't think would work. However, throughout my life, I failed at all of those endeavors because I lacked the formula, which I will share with you in this book. This formula will help you grow one profitable business, lighting the candle to financial freedom, lifestyle control, and greater impact in the world.

I hustled, and I hustled. I thought the key to success was just working harder, grinding, investing more time, money, and energy—but I was wrong about all those things. While all those things are a part of the success formula for any business, they are not foundational. They are important only after choosing the right business to grow based on your unique gift, which sets you apart from most businesses that fail.

Even after you discover your gift, you need a blueprint to design your brand in a way that attracts an audience to pay you attention and money! Without this blueprint, you may be tempted to follow another laid out process that doesn't align with the value you were created to bring the world. Hence, without following a system, it's too ambiguous and too uncertain.

Not to mention, every day, there is a new shiny object introduced to you as the key to how you're going to blow up. Somehow we believe it and fall into the trap of sinking more and more money into these "SUREFIRE" plans to build our wealth. What I learned time after time, as I invested time and money into different ventures over the years, is there is no magic system, bullet, or program that will transport me from poverty to wealth. Instead of studying another program or system, I discovered that studying myself was the foundational key to business success. Once I learned who I was and what I did naturally better than most people, I saw where I went wrong.

For example, the straw that broke the camel's back for me was a $15,000 investment I made into a real estate program. This program represented itself as a slam dunk wealth builder. Besides, real estate is responsible for making the most millionaires in the world. This industry is full of proven strategies for success, so I could not miss my wealth opportunity, right? Wrong! I bet on myself and sold out to the real estate coaching full time. After going hard for several months and following the coaching advice exactly, I ended up owing an additional $2,000 for deals that fell through. This left me feeling beat down and hopeless.

Still, I kept hearing in my heart that my gift will make room for me and bring me before great men. It was at that moment I committed never to neglect my gift ever again. Today, I stand here as an individual who stopped side hustling and made one business pop serving dozens of motivated paying entrepreneur clients in my growing coaching business. Now, I want to help you do the same. The philosophies and strategies are the key lessons I learned to make this happen, and I believe they can help you regardless of your gift or industry.

I'm so excited about your future and want to assure you that what you will learn has the power to take you from jack of all trades to focused master. As you go through this book, you will be able to digest and easily apply the information.

I'll give you the tools you need to be successful without holding back. You'll have the opportunity to access the resource library with all corresponding worksheets at bit.ly/infocusbookresources.

This book contains practical information, deliberate, intentional action steps, not just theory. It contains real-life experiences that will help you take immediate action and focus. It also helps to read this book with a friend or group of people who can hold you accountable while applying the book. Reading with others will incentivize you to put in the work and ride the momentum of your accountability to your success. Select a person or group that will not hold back in helping you. If you don't have a group or person to hold you accountable, feel free to join the Focus Academy community on Facebook at facebook.com/groups/rpfocusacademy

PART I
PURPOSE

CHAPTER 1

THE POWER OF YOUR GIFT

For you, this book might be the last straw. You may be saying I've tried everything, and, at this point, you're just curious to see what's inside this book. You may be feeling frustrated at a 9-5, knowing that your deepest desires are calling you to more. You may be overwhelmed with the process of starting a business endeavor because you simply don't know where to start. You may be a lifetime juggler of multiple businesses, hoping for one to work.

What if we could move from hoping to knowing? This is certainly possible. However, you will have to change your mind. Your mind will have to change from thinking your success is based on the quality of your business vehicle to your fit in the industry you pick. Also, it's not just about the industry you pick, but also how to deliver your product or service in the industry you choose. Regardless of the industry you choose, people are buying YOU after all. Let me say it this way.

"Poverty is not a problem. It is a result." - Dr. Myles Munroe.

A long time ago, I heard this quote from a world-renowned speaker who tragically passed away several years ago now. Let me break down this quote, facing the issue of poverty. Firstly, it's the result of you not knowing what your gift is. Secondly, it's the result of the world not knowing your gift.

If you know your gift—what you were genuinely and truly innately created to do—and people knew that of you, you can always attract resources into your life. When they think of you, they would think of something. And vice versa, when they think of something, they think of you. And that's really what you're going after—you want your name to be synonymous with something. This is what you want instead of being considered a jack of all trades and master of none. When you think of a jack of all trades, you don't think of something.

Some people would push back on this idea, saying that there are excellent examples of jack of all trades. Now I admit, some people are really talented at a lot of different things. However, if we trace it back to where they started, it began with one thing. I think of somebody like Beyonce. She has been able to act in films, produce fragrances, and own a clothing line. Still, she started with entertaining as a singer.

Singing is how we came to know her. That is her gift, and her gift made room for her. Therefore, we're starting here because I believe when a business pops, it has three things working. The first is purpose. Number two is priority, and number three is pace. This book addresses all three elements, but we will focus on the purpose arena in the next couple of chapters.

Priority comes into play after you know your purpose. You may know what you're supposed to be doing, but the question you have in this phase is: what order do I operate in to start building momentum on the movement I seek to create? What are the small details? How do I get going? Lastly, the pace area is all about tips, tricks, and tools that you learn along the journey to accelerate your results once you have a clear target and direction.

Let's address the purpose element in this chapter. We are starting here because we can't go out of order. If we start rushing ahead without firmly establishing purpose, we may end up somewhere we didn't bargain. So we have to start with purpose before we line up the other two.

Here's an analogy that may make it even clearer for you. Whenever I get in my car, and my internet is bad, the address in my GPS does not pop up, and I feel like I can't move. I can't go anywhere because I don't know which direction I'm going. In addition to that being true when we get in a car, it's also true in business. Sometimes, people focus on going a hundred miles an hour. They just focus on going really fast, when in reality, if you don't have an address in your GPS, you might just be wasting gas. Trying all of those businesses made me feel exactly like this is what I was doing—wasting gas and spinning my wheels like you may be doing right now.

If you continue down this path, you could end up nowhere really fast. Perhaps worse, you arrive at a place where you don't want to be. In my previous approach, speed was the goal, not a purposeful movement. That's why we have to start with this particular element.

There are three parts in this proven unique formula I created to help you discover your gift. The first ingredient to your gift discovery is childhood meditation. In thinking of childhood meditation, I think of my four-year-old son, Caleb. One of the things I love about my son is he's very extroverted. He's a leader, always getting other children to follow him, whether at school, church, or the playground. Wherever he goes, he likes to be the life of the party. If he grows up and does anything where maybe he's in a lab and not speaking to people, he would have missed his calling.

This trait was innately in him when he was born. I know this because my wife, a stay-at-home mom for the first couple of years of our marriage, has spent more time than I have with him since he was born. Since he spent more time with his mom, you would assume he would be introverted as my wife is extremely introverted.

Nonetheless, this is a nature-driven thing. There was something already on the inside of him when he came to earth. Going back to reflect on your childhood is the number one ingredient to discovering your gift. You can walk through some questions to get you engaged, such as, "When you got to earth, what things were true about you?" Life's experiences could be drowning out that reality, but I encourage you to walk back to it.

The number two ingredient to helping you discover your gift is data-driven self-awareness. The reason I say data-driven self-awareness is because an American study showed 95% of people believe that they're self-aware when only 15% actually are.

Assessments like the DiSC, Myers-Briggs, and Enneagram offer real results. These reports provide both sides of the coin for you. When you take them, you do not just receive information on all the great things about you but also the bad stuff about you. I used to have a pastor that would say, "The best thing about you is also the worst thing about you."

That's what these assessments help to show you. They show you a set of strengths and areas of growth. If you combine your focus on your childhood meditation with your data-driven self-awareness, you start to get a strong idea of who you are and what you're supposed to be doing.

The third and final piece to this puzzle is your personal and professional life experiences. This completes the puzzle and gives you your fingerprint. No matter how close in age you are to someone you have differences. You could have been twins with someone growing up in the same house, had the same parents, gone to the same schools, yet have entirely different experiences.

No one on this earth has the exact experience as you. This reality, coupled with childhood meditation and data-driven self-awareness, helps produce a beautiful puzzle that exposes your gift.

That's what you will work through in the first part of this book. Whether you have no idea what your gift is, or you simply want to crystalize the idea you already have, I'm excited that this is going to be able to happen for you! Be sure to complete the worksheets to ensure your best results.

To ensure you don't waste any more time without a clear sense of who you are and what you must bring to the world, I encourage you to go through this material with laser focus. Please take the free DiSC assessment at bit.ly/focusacademydisc to best complete the resources you will have access to throughout the book.

If you have any questions, feel free to book a complimentary call with me to discuss your assessment at bit.ly/rp30minchatchew.

When will you do your assessment? Now? No time right now? Be sure to plug it into your calendar as it will be a key to unlock the road ahead of you. Happy gift discovery!

Application:

1. Take the DiSC Assessment at bit.ly/focusacademydisc

CHAPTER 2

CHILDHOOD MEDITATION

This subject is near and dear to my heart because I believe it's the beginning of everything. Let me explain. Having a young son requires me to build several different toys. One thing I rely on heavily in building that stuff is the instructions that come in the instruction manual. These instructions are the mind of the manufacturer written down. This is how I equate reflecting on your childhood. I believe it provides a type of a manual as to what you were brought to earth to do. This is you before the world told you what career to go after or before your life experiences clouded the view of your true self.

Who you were as a small child contains instructions, direction, and guidance on who we should be as adults. The little us contains clues to why we were placed here, because what other explanation can you give for being brought here with certain characteristics? Some traits we learn as we grow and go through life, but there are other traits we're born with inside of us. For example, you were born right-handed or left-handed. You didn't have to work to receive this trait; it came with you when you got here.

A guy I know told me a story I'll never forget. He explained that his family kept making him put his spoon in his right hand to eat as a kid. However, he kept switching the spoon back to his left. This is contrary to what I think would naturally happen in this scenario. I thought he would eventually start eating with his right hand. However, it never happened. He just continued to eat with his left hand because he was left-handed—his instincts controlled how he behaved innately.

Hence, we came to earth with traits that give a clue, early in life, to what we were created to do. For example, if there's a kid who loves to play with Legos and build things more than anything else, that could give the child a clue to what he/she should spend his time doing as an adult. He should likely be building things or being involved in detailed work of some sort. A quote that embodies this trait was once said by Albert Einstein. He said, "Everybody is a genius, but if you judge a fish by its ability to climb a tree, it will live its whole life believing it is stupid."

Many people are involved in careers that are not fulfilling because of the concept behind this quote. You may feel like you are not the Michael Jordan of your industry because you are a fish right now trying to climb a tree. I'm so passionate about this lesson because it helps you recognize that if you were a fish, you should be in the water to be judged in the right element.

Also, relating to this quote, I think of the story of the famous actor, Denzel Washington. At the end of Denzel's first year of college, he had a 1.4 GPA, had no major, and didn't have much direction. The institution kindly asked him to leave because of how poorly he was doing in school. He talks about this being the lowest point of his life because he had no idea what he would do.

That summer, Denzel worked at a camp where he was placed over the campers' drama activities. He ended up doing well directing the campers and performing even better in his production role, prompting one of his friends to suggest that he should major in drama when he returned to school. That's precisely what Denzel did. Eventually, he went back to Fordham and majored in drama and journalism. The rest is history. Denzel became more than anyone could ever imagine in the film industry. I'm so glad that Denzel listened to his friend because he plays a pivotal role in many movies I love and was able to change his family's legacy.

As great as that story is, I have a newsflash for you. Before Denzel learned this gift was in him naturally, he was not working at acting. This wasn't a lifelong journey for him. He just so happened to do this at this camp and notice this gift was just within him. He wasn't trained for it, but he had it.

He later honed this skill with the training he put in, which has made him what he is today. But his friend's suggestion birthed Denzel Washington. While exciting, this scenario is dangerous because it appeared to happen by chance.

It was definitely inspired by God because I believe that nothing happens by chance. However, if you look at the situation, there wasn't an intentional and deliberate plan Denzel used to figure out his gift. It all miraculously came together.

Would you want to stumble upon this revelation as you never know how long something like that can take? On the contrary, would you prefer an intentional and deliberate plan, based on a process where you can much more predictably arrive at your gift? I would choose the latter, and I know you would too. The childhood meditation resource is accessible at bit.ly/infocusbookresources. This resource contains several childhood meditation questions that will begin to point you in the right direction of your gift.

Set aside at least 30 minutes to reflect on your childhood. Go back to the beginning.

What were you doing?

What were you focused on?

What did you do as a kid when you weren't doing anything?

What activities did you love to do in grade school?

What did friends, family, or teachers say you excelled at when you were a kid?

What school subjects did you enjoy most as a kid?

What clues do you get about your gift from the answer to these questions?

What is your child saying to you about how you were created and how you should invest your time daily? This will give you puzzle piece number one in this proven gift formula.

Application

1. Access and complete childhood meditation worksheet at bit.ly/infocusbookresources

CHAPTER 3

STRENGTH IDENTITY

A n American study showed that 95% of people believe that they are self-aware. However, through the same study, we learn that only 15% of people are actually self-aware. What that means is that without data-driven self-awareness assessments like the DiSC Assessment, Myers Briggs, or the Enneagram, it's hard to view ourselves objectively.

As it's really easy to deceive ourselves, here's what I suggest. Go to bit.ly/infocusbookdisc to take the free DiSC assessment. You will need to know your assessment information to personally relate the rest of the information shared in this chapter. I don't want you to make assumptions about yourself with the rest of what we'll go over. I want you to know for sure and be confident you are in the 15% of the self-aware people.

"If you are your authentic self, you have
no competition." - Scott Straten

I remember being at the gym, and as I looked in the mirror, I realized I started to be romantic about the progress that I was making. I looked at my stomach and realized I hadn't made as much progress as I thought I had, but I felt so much better. I'd been going to the gym for a couple of weeks and had begun to compare myself to others around me, but when I stepped on the scale, I realized not much had changed. I asked my wife, "babe, do I look different?"

She said, "Not really. You know, a little bit more muscular, but pretty much similar." That really hurt my feelings because I thought I'd been making significant progress. The reality was I was judging myself by looking in the mirror for what I needed.

That's why tools like the DiSC assessment are essential to help us view ourselves unbiasedly, like me looking at myself in the mirror. Here's a picture of the DiSC assessment through the lens of four jackets. You might have each jacket in your closet, but you do not wear them an equal amount of time throughout the year.

I know for me, my go-to is the hoodie. In the spring, I wear light hoodies. Also, on hot winter days and cool fall days, I wear hoodies.

I don't wear my winter coat as much. However, I do wear it when the wind is blowing hard, or it's snowing, and I need something aggressive and bulky.

The third jacket I wear rarely is the fall jacket. I wear the fall jacket when the winter coat is too heavy, and the hoodie is too informal or light.

The fourth is the summer rain jacket. I wear this one as a windbreaker if it's raining or for a chilly night by the water.

While each of these jackets can be well suited for certain occasions, they can be ill-fitting for others. The components of your DiSC assessment should be viewed in the same manner. One component is not better than another. Nonetheless, one character trait that we can tap into is going to be more appropriate for the weather or the circumstance that we're facing.

One movie I love and believe clearly exemplifies the DiSC is the Fantastic Four. The four characters in the Fantastic Four are the rock guy, the human torch, the invisible girl, and the stretch man. I encourage you to watch the movie, as you'll never see this assessment the same after watching it. I'm speaking of the version released in 2005 that includes the actors Ioan Gruffudd, Jessica Alba, Chris Evans, and Michael Chiklis.

The first person we want to look at is the D-type character. This character is the rock guy played by Michael Chiklis. I call him the driver. He is measured by the degree of dominance, defined as rule, control, authority. The symbol of this character is the fist. People like this are natural-born leaders, straightforward, fast-paced, energetic. They can be heard saying things like, "Do I have to do everything myself?" Famous D-types are Michael Jordan and Simon Cowell. Their focal point is decisiveness. The superpower of the D-type is that they give strength. These characters are great when it comes to penetrating a brick wall or a glass ceiling. If you ever get stuck on anything, this is the person you want in the foxhole with you. Can you think of a person like this, or is this you? What does your assessment say? In addition to the assessment, I want you to think about how you are connected to these character traits.

The next component of the DiSC is the I-type character. In the Fantastic Four, this person is the human torch played by Chis Evans. I call him the Inspirer. He is measured by his degree of influence. Influence is a compelling force on the actions, behavior, and opinions of others. The symbol of this character is fire. People like this are people-oriented, friendly, life of the party, and emotionally connected. They can be heard saying things like, "What if I don't want to be normal?" Famous I's are Oprah Winfrey and Will Smith. Their focal point is trust. The superpower of the I is they give spark. Can you think of a person like this, or is this you? What does your assessment say?

The next component of the DiSC is the S-type character. In the Fantastic Four, this person is represented by the invisible girl played by Jessica Alba. I call her the stabilizer. She is measured by her degree of steadiness, defined as being stable in position or equilibrium. The symbol of this character is the wind. People like this can be somewhat shy, with a lower sense of urgency. They prefer proven and traditional concepts. They can be heard saying, "We're going to be stuck here for a while, so let's try to get along." Famous S' are Michelle Obama and MLK. The focal point of the S-type is pace. The superpower of the High S is they give support. This is the person that really holds the structure together of an organization. This is the person that keeps the harmony within the group. Can you think of a person like this, or is this you? What does your assessment say?

The last component of the DiSC is the C-type character. In the Fantastic Four movie, this person is represented by the stretch man played by Ioan Gruffudd. I call him the calculator. He is measured by his degree of compliance, defined as cooperation or obedience. The symbol of this character is the brain. They can be heard saying things like, "My research suggests." People like this are suspicious of you and your solutions, do not make changes readily, and are not very talkative. Famous C's are Bill Gates and Warren Buffet. Their focal point is caution. The superpower of the C gives safety. These are the brainiacs behind the operations. They can do detailed work for long periods because they just have that research capacity. Can you think of a person like this, or is this you? What does your assessment say?

As we process this information, I want you to pull up your assessment and compare it to this sample assessment. I just want to explain to you what the bars mean. You have a color bar and a gray bar. The color bars are your natural behavior patterns, and the gray bars are your adaptive behavior patterns.

The best way to explain this is through the game of basketball. I'm in my natural state when I play on the court without thinking—I'm just shooting, passing, and dribbling based on my instincts. This typically happens when no one is at the game to observe me play, and I'm just going for it. That is my natural state. The color bars represent how I operate in my natural state.

Then, there are the gray bars. The gray bars are how I behave when I'm being observed, under stress or pressure. When I played basketball and my family came to the game, they were looking at me quite a bit, judging my actions. Whenever my Dad came to the game, I would feel an added level of pressure as I knew he would critique me after the game. These gray bars represent how I would act in a circumstance like that. You really want to pay attention to the instances where there is a large gap between the natural and the adaptive. This information tells a story based on the gap that exist. When natural and adaptive scores are similar within a behavioral component, there is little to no change in behavior when free or under pressure.

We have to figure out how to tell the story between when you're being natural and not thinking, compared to what happens with your actions when reacting to stressful situations. I really want you to look at your assessment. In the example of the assessment you see here, I would ask this individual to look at this chart on page two. This is the chart you see in figure 4.1. Simultaneously I would have them look at page 5. This is the chart you see in figure 4.2. which has the words on the chart that corresponds to the scores.

Figure 3.1

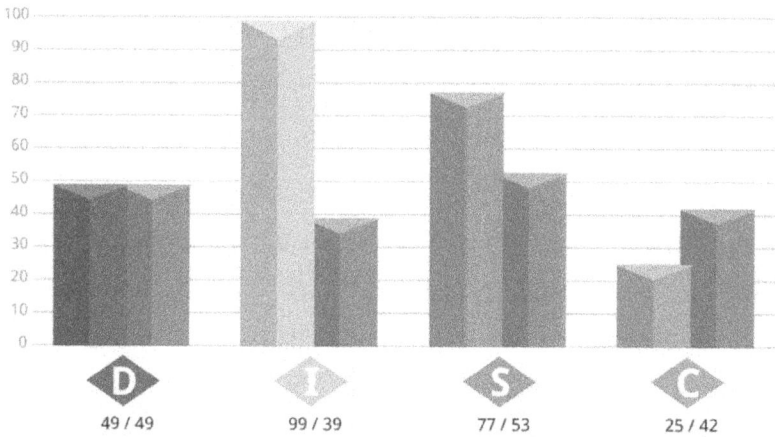

Figure 3.2

D	I	S	C
49 / 49	99 / 39	77 / 53	25 / 42

A closer look at the four components of your behavioral style

Decisive	Interactive	Stabilizing	Cautious
Problems:	People:	Pace:	Procedures:
How you tend to approach problems and make decisions	How you tend to interact with others and share opinions	How you tend to pace things in your environment	Your preference for established protocol/ standards
High D	High I	High S	High C
Demanding	**Gregarious**	**Patient**	**Cautious**
Driving	Persuasive	Predictable	Perfectionist
Forceful	Inspiring	Passive	Systematic
Daring	Enthusiastic	Complacent	Careful
Determined	Sociable	Stable	Analytical
Competitive	Poised	Consistent	Orderly
Responsible	Charming	Steady	Neat
Inquisitive	Convincing	Outgoing	Balanced
Conservative	Reflective	Restless	Independent
Mild	Matter-of-fact	Active	Rebellious
Agreeable	Reserved	Chaotic	Careless
Deliberate	**Introspective**	**Spontaneous**	**Challenging**
Low D	Low I	Low S	Low C

The scores don't mean much without the words defining the behavior pattern based on that score. Each word in the chart goes up on a continuum scale counting by 10 and excludes the bolded words at the top and bottom of the spectrum. For example, score 49 in the D column represents the behavior that corresponds with the word 'responsible' on the continuum. In the case of 49, you would just round up to 50.

Let's take things a step further. When you look at the decisive column, you see that it deals with problems and how you tend to approach problems and make decisions. The higher you are on the decisive spectrum, the more decisive and aggressive you are. The lower you are on this spectrum, the more agreeable and less decisive you are.

The I-type behavioral component measures your interactivity. It deals with how you tend to interact with others and share opinions. The higher you go on the I-type spectrum, the more trusting you are, and the more others trust you. The lower you go on that scale, the less trusting you are, and the less others trust you.

The S-Type behavioral component measures your pace. It's about how you tend to pace things in your environment. The higher you are on the S-type scale, the slower you like to pace things in your environment. The lower you are on the S-type scale, the faster you like to go. If you scored highest in this area and you're thinking to yourself, "oh no, I like to go slow"—let me explain further. You like to go slow yourself, and you are capable of slowing the game down for other people. This is a significantly powerful trait. If you've ever heard someone say, "Many people have taught this, but when you taught it, I truly understood it," that's the significance of a trait like that. This is certainly a superpower to embrace if that's you.

The C-type behavioral component measures your caution. This caution is a specific relationship to dealing with policies and procedures. The higher you are on this spectrum, the more cautious you are. The lower you go on this spectrum, the less cautious you are.

Take a look at figure 4.3. This chart here overlays the words and the scores. So you can see very clearly up here where this person scored close to a 50 D-type. Their natural and adaptive bars both land at the word responsible.

Figure 3.3

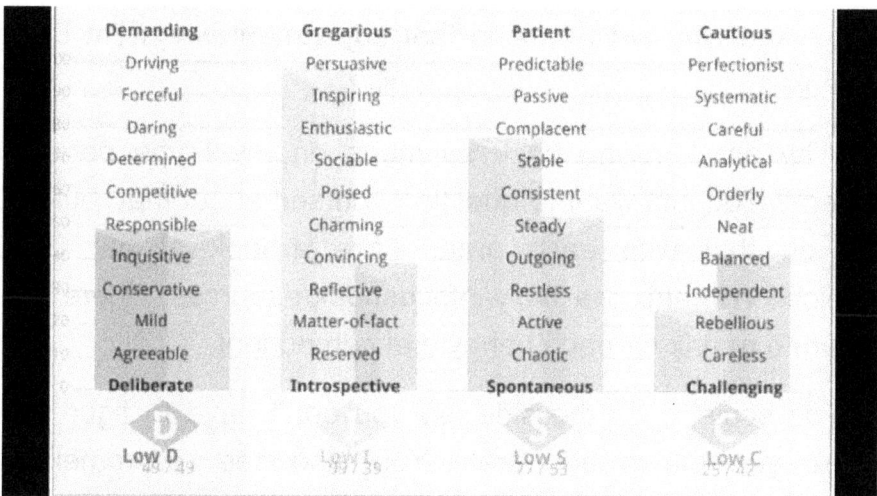

Demanding	Gregarious	Patient	Cautious
Driving	Persuasive	Predictable	Perfectionist
Forceful	Inspiring	Passive	Systematic
Daring	Enthusiastic	Complacent	Careful
Determined	Sociable	Stable	Analytical
Competitive	Poised	Consistent	Orderly
Responsible	Charming	Steady	Neat
Inquisitive	Convincing	Outgoing	Balanced
Conservative	Reflective	Restless	Independent
Mild	Matter-of-fact	Active	Rebellious
Agreeable	Reserved	Chaotic	Careless
Deliberate	Introspective	Spontaneous	Challenging

Low D   Low I   Low S   Low C

In the I-type category, the word that corresponds to the 99 natural score is persuasive. In comparison, the 39 adaptive score in this column lands on the word convincing. I would ask that the person look up the definition of persuasive through the DiSC Matrix you can find at bit.ly/infocusbookresources.

I would ask them where are you most likely pulling this trait from? Who did you learn this from throughout your life? Maybe a person or circumstance comes to mind, or maybe not. However, answering this question for each of your scores helps to tell the story where you see gaps.

The point of the question, nonetheless, is where is this coming from? Where have you seen this throughout your life? If you follow figure 4.3 in the I-type column down to the adaptive score of convincing, this individual would be best served asking when am I less trusting? What is happening there? From where am I pulling that trait? Where did I get that from? And why am I making that adjustment when I'm being observed?

Why am I pulling back so much on my I-type behavior pattern? You just want to question yourself about that, but you can do that with each area. Take a look at the DiSC Application Matrix via bit.ly/infocusbookresources. There is a separate matrix for each behavioral component.

The scale is on the side, so you don't have to figure out where you fall in any area. You also see recommended application questions for your natural scores. If you feel your adaptive score will have a greater impact on hitting your desired goals, you can ask the corresponding application question for that score. In this matrix, you will find the definitions for all the words and corresponding application questions. You have to find yourself based on your assessment in the matrix.

All these questions can be applied weekly, monthly, quarterly, and annually. Remember to maintain a running list of these answers as you go through the questions. Once you've taken your assessment, you can access another resource to bring clarity to your strengths at bit.ly/infocusbookresurces. This resource is 6 questions to help you understand your greatest strength and how to use it.

If you complete the activities to clarify your strengths, you will add a much-needed piece to the puzzle of discovering and crystallizing your gift. This should prevent you from going into a field or industry that does allow you to use your best assets in whatever you do, taking away your self-awareness advantage. This is a big component, is should lead to you no longer doing things that don't emphasize your strengths.

Application

1. Complete the DiSC Application Matrix for your greatest area of strength
2. Complete 6 Questions to Help You Understand Your Gift & How to Use it

CHAPTER 4

THE IMPROVEMENT GAP

———————o———————

Having an awareness of your areas for improvement is the first step to prevent yourself from building up with the one hand and tearing down with the other. Expert physicians say that the first step to overcoming a problem is admitting that we have a problem. That's where we want to start. I want to revisit the jacket analogy we covered in the last chapter. However, in this chapter, I'm going to cover the negative side of the jacket analogy.

Disadvantageous times when I wear my winter coat even in the wintertime is when I go to the mall with my wife. The winter coat ends up being too bulky to walk around in. It may be freezing outside, but I'm hot and really uncomfortable the entire time I'm in the mall. I might end up putting it underneath my child's stroller, feeling like if I just maybe wore a hoodie with a jacket on top, this situation could have played out a lot better.

On the other hand, there have been times when I've worn my fall jacket in the freezing cold and felt I really should've worn my Bubble North Face. The fall coat is good for the fall, but not the freezing cold winter in the northeast. This is especially true if the wind is blowing.

On the contrary, there are many times I've had on a hoodie when all I needed was a tee shirt. This happened to me recently, where I walked outside, and it seemed like it was a little chilly inside. But when I got out, I realized all I needed was a t-shirt. That's always annoying to have an unnecessary article of clothing with me, and in some situations, I just end up setting it down in a chair and losing the item.

Lastly, there are times I wear a summer jacket when I just need it to block the rain. However, I really don't want to have any extra clothing on when it's hot outside. I hate going to the movies with this type of jacket. With the air conditioner on, I end up freezing. In the end, I feel as though the summer jacket is not enough, and I should have brought a hoodie with me.

In all these cases, I explained jackets that are appropriate when they are appropriate, but inappropriate when they're inappropriate. These jackets paint a picture of how the right component used in an inappropriate element doesn't help at all. Therefore, I want to paint the dark side of the characters in the Fantastic Four from the previous chapter. We cannot build up with one hand and tear down with the other. That means you could be doing well in one area, but react negatively in other instances that cancel out the good side.

When I was a resident assistant (RA) in college, I came across two different kinds of resident assistant colleagues. One was great at community building, while the other was usually good at enforcing policies, procedures, and detailed work. The ones that were great at policies, procedures, and the detailed work weren't so great at community building and vice versa. Some people were a little bit more balanced, but for the most part, each RA was either a community builder or a policy enforcer. We see a correlation to this subject when we look at the four components of the DiSC assessment.

The D-type kryptonite is measured by your degree of unsteadiness, defined as not being steady or firm, being unstable, or shaky. People like this may seem harsh, impatient, and aggressive. They can be heard saying things like, "Do I have to do everything myself?" I remember Michael Jordan in his early years with the Chicago Bulls. He averaged 37 points a game in one season, but his team didn't win the championship. One reason is he was trying to do everything, and it wasn't until he grew to the point where he started to trust his teammates that he began to win championships. The focal point is a fast pace. Their kryptonite causes division. When you're breaking through walls all the time, breaking through ceilings, achieving things at a high level, there will always be people that are going to be casualties in the process. Due to a lack of compassion or empathy these people could exhibit when they go too far in the immature direction, they may not be rich in friendships. Can you think of a person and a situation where you've felt this from someone in your life? Is this person you?

Before I break down the other three components, I want you to think of each of these, like cooking broccoli. If you're too much of who you are unapologetically without thinking, and without processing your environment, then you run the risk of being too soggy. No one wants soggy broccoli. But if you're not enough of who you are, you run the risk of being too hard, crunchy, and undercooked. What we're after is broccoli cooked just right in the sweet spot. This is the mature approach to each DiSC component.

The next DiSC component is the I-type. The I-type kryptonite is measured by their degree of incompliance defined as not compliant, unyielding. People like this may seem lazy, unproductive, and slick-talking. They must be reminded, "With great power comes great responsibility." The focal point is negligence. Their kryptonite causes destruction.

You can have a power current when on that is so powerful it is inspiring. When it is not needed, that same power can blow out whatever the mechanism is because it's just too powerful. This is me. I'm an I-type. So what I must recognize is when I'm communicating with someone who needs facts and figures, they don't need inspiration. I can't go too far in the direction of inspiration because then I'll break that person's current. If I pay attention more in certain instances and am more cautious, I avoid certain headaches. Therefore, I need to keep people in my life who create systems and prevent me from going too far in the wrong direction. Can you think of a person and a situation where you've felt this from someone in your life? Is this person you?

Next, we have the High S-types. Their kryptonite is measured by their degree of powerlessness, defined as the inability to produce an effect, helplessness. People like this may seem indecisive. They must be reminded that "if not now, when?". The focal point of the S-type is indecision. Their kryptonite causes stagnation. This is the person who sometimes feels like life is happening to them versus them having to chase their dreams. This person typically feels they support everyone else and have nothing left for themselves. I would tell this person that you could have an opportunity to do yours if you took a step back and decided what was necessary and what wasn't necessary for the moment. That thought process alone could create a different outcome.

Here's a story. I had family members who didn't go to church for some time. Another family member told me that these people couldn't go to church because they didn't have transportation. I said to myself, these people can't go to church because they are not figuring out a way to go. It sounded harsh at the time, but what the person soon realized is that what I was saying was true. The next week after we had that conversation, I assumed those family members didn't go to church. Then, to my surprise, the person told me they went. They just took an Uber. I thought to myself, that is my point EXACTLY.

It's just like how we would make things happen if we had a job interview coming up. We would make it happen. This person needed to be reminded of this principle. Can you think of a person and a situation where you've felt this way from someone in your life? Is this person you?

Lastly, we have the C-type person. Their kryptonite is measured by their degree of skepticism, defined as doubt or unbelief. People like this may seem slow, stubborn, and overwhelmed with too many questions. They must be reminded at times, "If you think long, you think wrong." The focal point is distrust. Their kryptonite causes fear. Think about it; if a person is always thinking about all the things that can go wrong religiously, they will get to a point where fear paralyzes them. The crazy part of fear is that it's mostly a false sense of reality. Can you think of a person and a situation where you've felt this from someone in your life? Is this person you?

This is the concept of the kryptonite. You might be thinking, what is my kryptonite? We looked at how to determine your strength in the previous chapter; now, we will look at a person's kryptonite in an example. **Figure 4.1**. According to this example, the I-type is their highest natural score and where their superpower comes from with a score of 99. On the other hand, their kryptonite is their C reflected by the blue column score, which is their lowest score. It's 25.

Figure 4.1

Demanding	Gregarious	Patient	Cautious
Driving	Persuasive	Predictable	Perfectionist
Forceful	Inspiring	Passive	Systematic
Daring	Enthusiastic	Complacent	Careful
Determined	Sociable	Stable	Analytical
Competitive	Poised	Consistent	Orderly
Responsible	Charming	Steady	Neat
Inquisitive	Convincing	Outgoing	Balanced
Conservative	Reflective	Restless	Independent
Mild	Matter-of-fact	Active	Rebellious
Agreeable	Reserved	Chaotic	Careless
Deliberate	Introspective	Spontaneous	Challenging
Low D	Low I	Low S	Low C

If we look at the chart here, we can see that the score lands between 20 (rebellious) and 30 (independent). You would read the definition to each word to determine which word most naturally connects with how you operate in that area. The power is in identifying the exact word that exemplifies the character trait, which allows you to develop a prescription for that kryptonite. The recommended questions in the DiSC Application Matrix are designed to lead you to practical solutions for that improvement gap.

You can also access six questions to help you understand your kryptonite and how to contain it at bit.ly/infocusbookresources. You will need to have completed the DiSC assessment to be able to answer the questions.

In looking at your kryptonite, be cautious of devoting all your energy and resources to making this area better while neglecting your strengths. John Maxwell once said that if you are a three in an area, you should not work hard to become a five. I thought, why? This seems pretty noble. He explained that people still don't pay if you become a five in an area. Instead, he recommended improving where you are a seven or eight to a nine or ten. People pay for mastery, not average.

So here's what I recommend to do with your areas of improvement. Delegate, automate, or eliminate what you don't do well naturally. This system truly provides the prescription for the areas in your life that would otherwise block you from success. For instance, my assessment says that I'm best served when I only touch things one time. At the time I learned this, I sent invoices to all my clients. It's sad to say that some clients fell through the cracks, and I lost money because of my lack of follow-through at times on this strategy. Because of this pain point, I instituted a payment system that I only had to set up once, and all clients started paying through a link I would send them. Also, the system is subscription-based; therefore, it is automatically done for me, and I only have to touch it once.

Based on the same negative traits, I pay a virtual assistant every month to manage my course platform and online group customer service. However, my secret sauce is eliminating the work that doesn't move the needle to my bottom line or fit my strength. As an entrepreneur, you must remember you are not required to do everything, and your customers will typically adjust to the guidelines and boundaries you set. We know Chic-Fila is not open on Sundays. Therefore, we just consume it on any day but Sunday. Even though it may be disappointing when you have a taste for it on Sundays, this is a boundary we respect as customers of the restaurant. You must set the same boundaries for your business because you must know what you do not do as much as you know what you do. If it doesn't work for you, eliminate it.

Application

1. Complete The DiSC Application Matrix for your greatest area of improvement
2. Complete 6 Questions to Help You Understand Your Kryptonite & How to Contain It

CHAPTER 5

THE EXPERIENCE TOOLBOX

I n this chapter, we look at your personal and professional experiences. This includes your skills, knowledge, and other things you've gained over the years. Afterward, we will look at how they complement your core traits with which you were born. All the components work together to form a complete puzzle.

Here's what I know to be true; your personal and professional experience is like your fingerprint. You're the only one who has it. When it comes to your gifts, this is the greatest separator and the reason someone can do exactly what you do and not take up all the slots. There is someone attracted to your voice, your way of doing things, your way of looking at things. Someone else may be from a similar socioeconomic background, but your voice may resonate with an individual more. Never discount this by believing the lie that the market is too saturated to house another successful entrepreneur. If it's your gift, there's nobody who does it quite like you.

I think about my two cousins growing up. They were twins. They had the same parents, same household, same family. Yet, they had different personalities, different ways they went about their business, different ways they approached their schoolwork, different ways they approached the sports they played, different ways of living life. Everything was so different, even though they were born in the same place at the same time.

It doesn't matter how similar your experiences are to someone else; it is not the same. That's what I love about the beauty of your experience. Check out the questionnaire that allows you to take a deeper dive into your life experience at bit.ly/infocusbookresources.

Here are the questions:

1. What were your parents' or guardians' professions growing up? How did they shape your worldview?
2. Were you raised as an only child, or did you have siblings? If you had siblings, what order were you born?
3. What skills did you develop as a result of your birth order?

I think of a woman who is the oldest of four who took on caretaking roles from a very young age. She was responsible for cooking, cleaning, and different things around the house. Older people usually do these chores, but it helped her develop responsibility and maturity. She's an exemplary caretaker at this point, but that experience shaped her.

1. What city did you grow up in and attend high school?

2. What was the socioeconomic status of where you grew up and attended high school? What skills have you developed as a result of being in this environment?

3. What is your faith background? What values do you have as a result of your faith background?

4. What is your professional work experience? What skills, knowledge, and expertise have you gained as a result?

5. What is your marital status? Are you a parent? If so, how many children do you have? What advantages do you have as a result of this experience?

6. What is the highest level of education you've experienced? What was your academic area of focus? What knowledge, skills, or expertise do you have as a result?

Bonus question: What is your why or motivation for your life goals? What excites you? What most angers you? I love that question. What most angers you?

I remember majoring in filmmaking in college because I really hated the movies that I watched. I hated the some stories and the lack of stories within the movies I watched. And that's the reason I majored in film. It was always so funny to explain that to people, as they usually were like, "Really? You major in film because you hate it?" I would smile and say, "yes, that's exactly right." Well, I didn't ultimately go into film, but it did drive me to excel at it in college.

If you choose to think about them and go inside yourself with your answers, this will be another major puzzle piece in determining your unique advantage in the marketplace. Everything you need is in your hands—dig deep.

Application:

1. Complete 9 Personal & Professional Questions to Help You Determine Your Gift

CHAPTER 6

FAMILY SURVEY

———————o———————

As you go through life, you have ups and downs and can sometimes have really positive and negative experiences with your family. However, this particular lesson focuses on your family being with you for a long period of your life in many cases. Due to the length of time with your family and lifelong friendships, they will be able to point out personal strengths that you may naturally overlook. It can be easy to overlook what we are best at because we are naturally not impressed by it. So we search. Have you ever run into someone who had an extraordinary talent, and you pointed it out to them, and they felt like it was nothing?

Have you had a frustrating moment like this in the past? What were your thoughts? Were they "how can you not see how valuable this thing is"? Well, here's what I want to let you know. Some people are looking at you in the same way. There are things you do well naturally—but pay it no mind—that people could only hope and dream of doing as well as you.

This normally happens when we are comparing ourselves with others. You may be too busy looking at where you are, where you want to be, where others are, but this chapter will help you open your eyes and see yourself in ways that you may be overlooking.

With this in mind, I'm reminded of my family. My grandparents started this tradition where we celebrate Christmas and Thanksgiving on one day. This was a solution they came up with so that our immediate families aren't split up on either Christmas or Thanksgiving. This past holiday season, we played a game called White Elephant. A rule of thumb in this game is that most people tend to go for the really small envelopes because the really small envelopes usually have gift cards in them.

Therefore, the larger boxes tend to get overlooked. I remember being devastated when we played last. There was a huge box that someone grabbed, and people overlooked it because everyone was going for the small items. To our surprise, this package had an amazing duffle bag inside. It was a travel duffle bag with wheels, to be exact. It was the perfect size as well, not too bulky.

It was like a dream come true of a bag. It was in this huge box, but there was also a gift card in the box. At this point, I was blown away. One of the most phenomenal white elephant gifts ever.

The beauty was in the box. This is what I'm saying about you. There is beauty inside your box. Sometimes it takes people closest to you to point it out. This person may not be a family member from a relative standpoint, but someone really close to you who has known you for a long time. They would be able to speak to certain positive traits you possess.

I remember I asked a friend of mine this question—what comes easy to me but is hard for most people? I asked it two other ways as well. I said when I walk into a room, what walks in? You could also ask the question: What do I do best with the least amount of effort? Asking the question in these different ways may help get the respondent to produce the most meaningful response.

Upon asking my friend, I received a magical answer because he shared something with me that I never previously consciously thought. Yet, it rang true to me when he said it.

He said, "I think what walks in when you walk in is your perspective. You offer a really unique perspective that gives people a different way of looking at things and provides meaningful clarity to how they should move forward with that information. It helps to move people from point A to point B." For instance, in college, a few of my friends and I would go to the campus diner and have really deep conversations. When we were there, we would be up all night to like two or three o'clock in the morning, just talking, having deep conversations at the diner. Most times, as the conversation was concluding, my friends would look at me as if to say, tell us what this means. What does this mean for our lives? And what do we do about it? On cue virtually every time, I would answer through analogies and my unique perspective that provided clear direction for everyone at the table.

This gave me a clue to help steer me in the direction I'm in now, assisting individuals to gain clarity about their business direction and how to best approach their venture. I help people sum things up and give the next steps. My friend was able to show me that, and it changed my life. Never neglect the power of asking the right questions!

I no longer compare myself to people who have other gifts that I admire. For instance, my mentor has massive energy on stage; he just commands the stage, getting people excited and inspired to move. I've tried to do that; it never quite works as well for me. I could only do it in spurts because it's not my gift. Once I realized it's my unique perspective that I can use to move people. I started to exercise it, which is the single revelation that began to help me really build and explode my business. I want you to share in this experience, so here's what I want you to do. Access & complete the family gift survey questionnaire at bit.ly/infocusbookresources.

You're going to survey your family/close friends and ask them this question. What comes easy to you that's hard for most people? This activity is the last piece of your gift puzzle. It's truly going to bring everything together you've been working on up until this point. The unique formula combination of childhood meditation, data-driven self-awareness, personal and professional experience, and the evaluation of your family gift survey should give you a clear picture of your gift.

You'll be able to tie a bow on this and move on to designing your brand around your gift once complete. The statement I want you to produce will come by completing Your Gift Display worksheet at bit.ly/infocusbookresources. The thing I do best with the least amount of effort is filling in the blank. You will write that out on the worksheet, and we'll be one step closer to you discovering your gift and growing a profitable business from it!

Realizing who you are and what you're supposed to be doing can be extremely liberating, and I'm genuinely excited for you!

Remember your gift makes room for you and brings you before great men. - Proverbs 18:21

Hang your gift display completed worksheet on your wall and commit never to neglect to do this daily again. I'm going to encourage you to take it a step further—share it publicly with people who are like-minded and will hold you accountable for using it.

You now know how to discover your gift without wasting more time! I can't wait to see the impact you make with those you influence by using your gift and changing your family trajectory and financial potential!

Application:

1. Complete the Family Gift Survey
2. Complete Your Gift Display Worksheet

CHAPTER 7

THE SCIENCE OF MARKET SELECTION

N ow that you've successfully discovered your gift or got a lot closer, it's all about deciding on a business where you can target customers who are already in the market for your offer.

It's not about you as an entrepreneur. You must think like a fish and not a fisherman.

Remember, the customers are the fish. As an entrepreneur, you are the fisherman. However, you have to think like the fish, not the fishermen.

You must know what fish like to hear, see, smell, taste, and feel. You must learn them because you're not trying to catch yourself. You already have yourself. I know that may sound corny, but it's true. You already know your thoughts. You already have the income that you have; you already have the life that you have.

You should be thinking, "What must get out of your head and into the customer's mind, so you can build a profitable business that guarantees you results?"

There was a time when I was thinking just like a fisherman. When I first went into business, I started a business based on student staff training. The first thing I learned was college students were not motivated customers for independent contract training. They're just trying to graduate from school. This may be a cool thing on the weekend during training here and there, but it really wasn't something they were concerned about year-round.

From a professional standpoint, they were training the staff normally, so they didn't really have the urgency to hire me. I spent several years in student affairs. I was focused on the fact that I had mastered the skills of training and presenting over the years of working with these students. I had skills like training and presenting, and therefore, I should just make it a business, right?

There was one problem. This approach was all about me. It was about the experience I had and what I wanted to give. It was just about me. I felt like I was tremendously helpful. However, all of that didn't matter because I was not thinking like a fish, which left me busy, fishing in a pond with very few fish.

All this changed one day when I attracted a motivated fish. Here's how it happened. I was in a daily accountability group. We did a one-hundred-day challenge. I was responsible for texting different individuals to alert them of the completion of my goals every day. In my being consistent, I never really got anything back from most of my accountability partners. Part of me said to myself, just stop texting them. Until one day, one partner said to me, "Hey, are you a coach?" I thought to myself, well, I'm not currently coaching one-on-one clients. However, since you're inquiring, I'm open to hearing what your needs are, and maybe I can help.

I reached out to the individual who told me what area they needed help. As far as what this individual needed help with, I could help because I was doing it. This person simply wanted to achieve their daily personal goals at a higher rate than they were experiencing. This person became my first individual coaching client and started to teach me how fish heard, saw, smelled, tasted, and felt by showing me the things they needed help with, like procrastination and other issues.

With this, I began to listen to other people and where they would say they need help. People were saying things like, "I set these goals, and I don't get them accomplished." At this moment, the light bulb went off in my head! I used to struggle with procrastination. I don't anymore! I've reached a point in my life where I am keeping the promises that I make to myself at a high rate. So why don't I help people do that? This was a genius idea at the time because I branded myself as the productivity coach and drew several other clients to me without really having any sort of marketing campaign. It was all word of mouth.

I just kind of put myself out there, letting people know who I am and what I do. The next thing I knew, I had clients coming to me. At this point, I realized, why keep trying to struggle to attract student staff training clients when people were already coming to me for something else? If I chose to help individual paying clients with things like procrastination, I could control my own destiny. That decision turned out to be genius because those one-on-one clients turned into group coaching clients, eventually leading me to other business doors opening.

I will be welcomed into larger corporate settings based on the brand that I've developed personally. I was the same guy with the same level of talent and expertise. However, where I directed my talent and expertise made all the difference and the money. It made me realize whenever you're creating a successful business, it's not just about your creativity and your ideas, but it's also about the fish. Do they want what I'm offering? Are they truly motivated to get it? In other words, is there already a motivated market?

This experience opened my eyes to the deadliest mistake many entrepreneurs make on the journey to building a profitable business and paints the philosophy of how I want you to think throughout this book and beyond. I want you to think like a fish.

Application

1. After going through this chapter, on a scale from 1-10, how would you rate yourself on thinking like a fish?
2. What are 3 ways you can you begin to think more like a fish in your business?

3. Who can you connect with who has consistently demonstrated the ability to attract fish (customers) to gain ideas in this area?

CHAPTER 8

CHOOSING THE RIGHT MARKET

I cannot say this enough, as an entrepreneur, you must think like a fish and not a fisherman. This thought process should provoke the question, what are people already looking for? I was faced with this question in graduate school as I was tasked to design a t-shirt for intramural sports champions. I used a Flyer Than Most Nike t-shirt as my example. At the time, many people were wearing Nike t-shirt with all kinds of sayings on campus. You may be familiar with these Nike t-shirts and may have seen people wear them over the years.

Instead of coming up with an original design that I felt was fabulous that no one else thought was attractive, I used the fish philosophy. I looked at students around campus and the shirts that they were already wearing. Then I said to myself, I'm going to create a shirt that looked almost identical to the Nike shirt because that's what students were already looking for. I used the same font as the Nike shirt. It's called Futura, by the way. I just added some Wolverine eyes and the words Wesley College underneath the featured letters on the shirt. I call this practical market research.

The question you may have is how to do this practically in your business as an entrepreneur without doing a bunch of surveys. The reason I bring up perhaps using alternative measures of evaluations to surveys is sometimes you want to be strategic and cautious with sharing your ideas.

I don't know this to be totally true, but I ran a survey one time while living in Delaware. The survey was to gauge interest for a miniature golf course as there was no miniature golf courses within an hour driving distance of Dover, Delaware.

A few of my buddies and I were going to start a miniature golf course in town. However, less than one year after that survey, one popped up in the area. It could've been based on that survey, or the person could have had an original thought. Still, that's the danger—you never know.

However, I learned of a tool about a year ago that allows you to get feedback on an idea without running an arbitrary survey that may not produce reliable results depending on the sample size and demographic surveyed. This tool is called Google Trends. It allows you to see the rate people are searching for things in google all over the world. Now that's efficient!

In the book, "Choose," author Ryan Levesque introduces this tool as a way to test business ideas against this trend he found in 23 of the multimillion-dollar businesses he built. He explains that the differences he saw in the successful businesses and those that flopped was this trend. He explains that the successful businesses fell in a range of trends he called evergreen markets. These businesses were searched frequently enough to be considered viable, but not so much that the new entrepreneur could drown in the market.

He uses the example of these evergreen markets to set the range of the sweet spot you want your business to fall into. He gives the example of Orchid Care, Improve Memory, Leadership Skills, and Beekeeping as evergreen markets as seen in **figure 8.1**. Without providing a masterclass lesson on using Google Trends, I will show you how to use this tool to test your business idea right here properly.

Figure 8.1

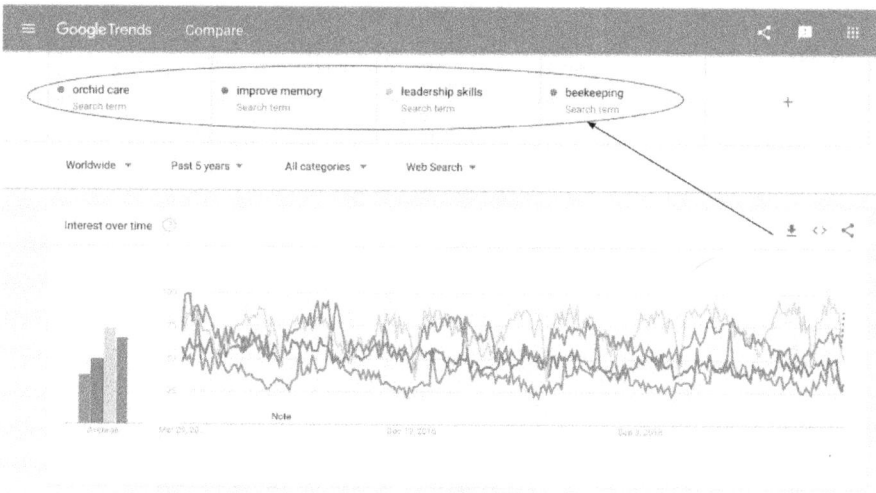

In his book, "Choose," Ryan Levesque provides a masterful breakdown on Google Trends if you want to go deeper. The question we are trying to answer is, what are people already looking for? You don't want to pick something too large like the market Levesque started with, which was 'Orchid.' He realized it was too big and did not fit the evergreen trend, so he niched down to 'Orchid Care,' and it fell right in the sweet spot.

However, you also don't want to pick a too small a market or where there's no market for it at all. You want to make sure that your search is set to the following filters: worldwide & the past five years. You want to do this to ensure a trend isn't fly by night and just started recently, but also you don't need to go too far back if the market has been consistently viable for five years and is here to stay.

If you plug the term 'Orchid' in the search with our correct filters, it towers over the other sweet spot markets in the example I gave as seen in **figure 8.2**. This communicates an over-saturated market. What you want to do is niche down until your search can get in the sweet spot.

Figure 8.2

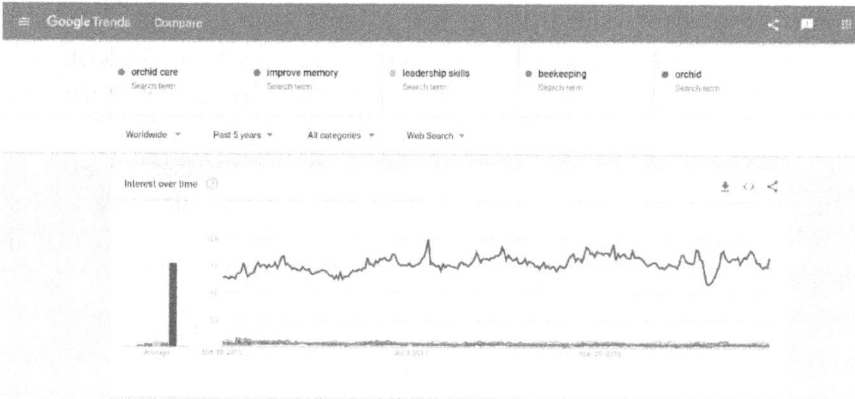

To see a market that's too small, let's look at the market I started with—student staff training. This is the opposite of when we add orchid on this search—with this, it's really low. In other words, I was trying to build a business without any fish. No matter how great my marketing, products, or content was, the fish just simply not searching for me as seen below in **figure 8.3**.

Figure 8.3

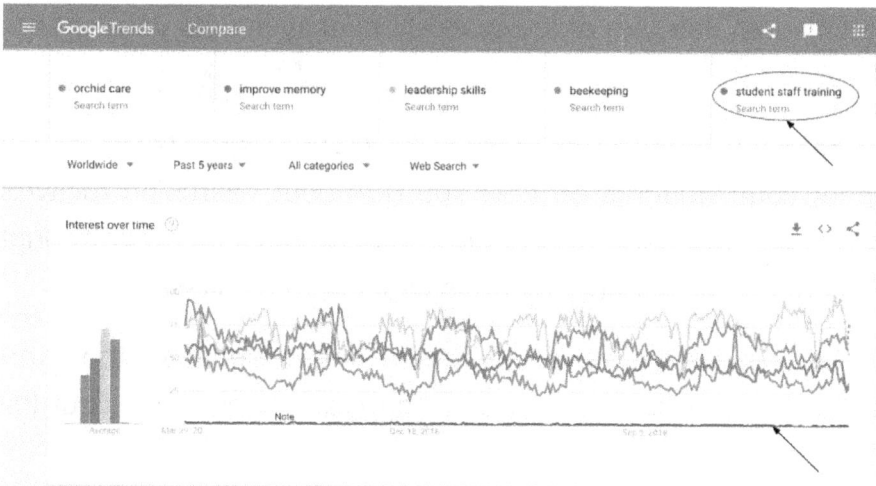

A market that falls right in the sweet spot is what I'm doing now as a business coach. This is right in the range you want your business to fall. It's right in line with the other evergreen trends. You are halfway to success when you pick the right market to target! To drastically raise your chances of success in business, you must aim to attract a market already looking for what you do and is evergreen. Cha-Ching! Check out the difference in **figure 8.4** below.

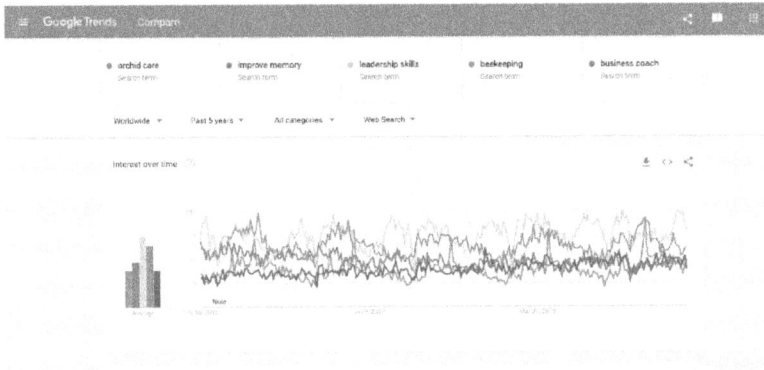

As I mentioned earlier, Ryan Levesque has built several multimillion-dollar businesses that fit within this sweet spot on a worksheet you can find at bit.ly/infocusbookresources, which has an example of about 25 evergreen markets according to google trends. Use this sheet as a guide to frame your idea. Heck, even use one of the markets exactly if it fits your gift and expertise.

However, even if it doesn't fit exactly, that list can kind of spark your thoughts on how you go about searching for what you want. Choosing the right market worksheet goes through setting this up without any guesswork step by step.

I'm not saying never to run a survey because there are many times when surveys done right are appropriate, but this tool is a way to have total confidence that what you're doing aims at an evergreen market! Happy testing!

Application:

1. Complete the Choosing the Right Market Worksheet

CHAPTER 9

ESTABLISHING YOUR BRAND VISION

Do you know why everyone says,
don't judge a book by its cover?

Becase it's what we instinctively do, people judge books by the cover. With that in mind, I want to focus on your book, which is your brand in this scenario. When I say your brand/business cover, I'm talking about your website.

When I started my business, people would ask me, so what do you do exactly? And I would fumble over several lines, even though I knew exactly what I did. However, I didn't have a polished version that drew people to my cover. So I want you to solidify an attractive cover.

Before you take off down the road, I want you to pause for a second as you must first establish the foundation that determines your direction and desired lifestyle alongside your business. I want you to think about your number one goal for your business and your brand. I want you to think about the lifestyle you want, the time freedom, the financial freedom, and the amount you want to earn annually.

The reason we start here is if you come up with a viable business brand, but then you don't love operating it, then that is not a win for you or others around you. For instance, if you say you want to own a restaurant. However, what goes into owning and operating a restaurant is getting your hands dirty 24/7. You may make a lot of money but not be happy with your life. You want to establish your brand based on the overall life pitcher you want to create.

Take a deep breath. Take a step back. Envision what you want. Then begin crafting your vision for moving towards it. Let's do this now. Three to five years from now, what do you want this brand that you're establishing to lead to for yourself and your loved ones?

Think about your lifestyle, time freedom, financial freedom, and who you want to be. I have some questions to help you map that out and the brand vision worksheet at bit.ly/infocusbookresources. Here's an example of how mine reads.

Thanks to my online business, I'm able to spend time with my wife and kids every day at whatever time of day I choose. I am a well-respected author, coach, and sought after speaker for business opportunities all across the United States.

Every day I'm faced with new questions that inspire me to grow in my field. I'm a multimillionaire. My wife has the freedom to spend what she pleases, while my team and I can follow our organization's calling without stressing about cash flow or paying the bills. I'm elated I started this journey just a few short years ago!

Again, you're going to see the questions that will prompt you to come up with this statement on your own for your brand. This is a major key to your success as it will provide direction for your business as far as what you say yes and no to as you're building. Without completing this step, you might build a great business, but a life you hate. My goal is to help you do both, create a dream business alongside your dream lifestyle.

Application:

1. Complete the Brand Vision Worksheet

CHAPTER 10

ESTABLISHING YOUR BRAND ASSETS

———————o———————

A mentor of mine told me a story regarding a Sprite can. He was talking to a corporate organization, where he held a Sprite can up and asked, "What is in this container?" They responded with things like lemon, lime, and acid. All of which was true.

However, the word he was looking for was liquid, which someone eventually gave to him. Then he said, "What makes the liquid in the Sprite can valuable is that it is packaged, contained, branded, and can be purchased for commerce."

"Your problem is that you are liquid as well, but you're all over the place." By this, he meant, you have value inside you, ready to ooze out of you, but it's not until you package it in a way where people can pinpoint what you're for that your value can be brought to the marketplace for business.

This scenario reinforces the issue we see in a previous chapter that says, "Poverty is not a problem, it's a result." -

Myles Munroe. Now that you know what your gift is and you know you must package it in exchange for commerce, let's make it happen!

That's what the rest of this chapter is all about. It's about providing you with a guide in a few simple steps that do not take all year to complete. There are a few simple steps for you to establish your brand and your brand assets. When you're able to do that, you solve the poverty problem! You solve the poverty problem not just from a financial standpoint but from a life fulfillment standpoint. Plenty of people making a tremendous amount of money are just not using their gifts to do it, and therefore are not fulfilled.

They're not in the 15% who are happy with their careers, jobs, or businesses. Once you crack this code, you'll be able to enter that world. The first thing that you must do is establish your brand identity. You'll find the worksheet you can access to establish your brand identity at bit.ly/infocusbookresources.

The worksheet will help you work out everything I'm going to mention for you. Another way of thinking about your brand identity is your value proposition statement. This statement should plainly state your professional identity, who you help, what do you help them do or understand, and the promised or desired outcome they'll receive through doing business with you. This statement can always be reworked or retooled, but for now, it needs to be done.

The next level is letting people know how you help them. This is usually through 1-3 main mediums of communication or service that you choose. My three examples would be curriculum, coaching & camps. However, the value proposition statement is the statement that draws potential customers in so they can become curious about your how.

It's funny they call it an elevator pitch because if you imagine being on the elevator with someone, you have a quick moment to make a great impression in the conversation. From here, you will establish your tagline, which is shorter than the value proposition statement but still gets people excited about the transformation you offer. The tagline typically grows out of the value proposition statement. You can take the juiciest part of the value proposition statement to create your tagline, which is usually ten words or less.

For example, my value proposition statement is, "I'm Robert Price - Business Coach. I help serial entrepreneurs stop side hustling & make one business pop."

My tagline is: Helping You Stop Side Hustling & Make One Business Pop!

Another thing that helps you think of your brand's clarity, in a nutshell, is your brand descriptives. When you think about McDonald's, one of the first words to come to mind is value. McDonald's is all about real estate, having as many places as possible surrounding you to where you cannot defeat it because it's all based on value. Then, there are other companies we can think of like Amazon, who's big and their word is speed.

They're all about speed and efficiency. Now I want you to think about what are going to be your words. Within what you do, what do you want people to know you for? Is your brand friendly, welcoming, innovative, modern, or classic? You can access the brand descriptives worksheet at bit.ly/infocusbookresources.

The next important thing to consider is your brand colors. Your brand colors should grow out of your brand descriptives. When we look at Google, we see color, the blue, the red, the yellow, and the green. When you think about Google, this is the image that you get in your mind. These colors include the primary colors, which show their value of teamwork, and the one secondary color, which shows their value of individual brilliance.

Now I want you to think about your brand colors. There's a worksheet and some resources there to help you think through your brand colors at bit.ly/infocusbookresources. Whether you want them to be focused, exciting, or fun, your colors should represent your brand descriptives when you think of your words.

Next, are your brand photos. When beginning a business, your photo is truly your logo. People connect with people, after all. Take one day and hire a photographer to take photos of you. It doesn't have to be expensive. It could even be a good friend with a nice camera. Check out the photo shoot checklist at bit.ly/infocusbookresources to find all poses you will need for your website, marketing campaigns, and sales pages.

When you take things a step further beyond your brand vision, your descriptives, colors, and messaging need to be tight. Bill Clinton once said you need a 30-second, 5-minute, and 20-minute version of your message. I thought this was profound because even though you're not necessarily going to craft a 30-second, 5-minute, and 20-minute version of your message, it is important to think about what you are communicating in these terms.

In practical terms of expanding your value proposition statement and your tagline, the next layer of your messaging is your brand bio. This is a more expanded version of what you want people to know about who you are, who you help, what you do, and your promised outcome. There's an example of a strong brand bio at bit.ly/infocusbookresources. As there is nothing new under the sun, I recommend not reinventing the wheel. You could simply follow the structure of the example brand bio and plug in information specific to you and your brand.

When writing your brand bio, there are a few things you want to keep in mind. First, write your bio in the first person. You want to be sure your message is personal. You want to talk to your potential customers directly. You want it to be conversational. You want to address the reader's priorities right away. Tell them about yourself and inform them of your consistent lead magnet. Many people need to touch what you do several times before they ever make a decision to purchase. Set an expectation of where and when they can find you delivering value consistently.

Invite them to take a step. Provide a link to a full bio and then share the best way to contact you. Here's the example.

Hello, I'm Robert Price, a passionate business coach. My goal is to help serial entrepreneurs stop side hustling and make one business pop. After walking away from my 7+ years career as a student affairs professional, I launched my consulting business because I wanted more income, more freedom, and more impact.

Since transforming from student affairs professional to a work-from-anywhere business consultant, I've worked with dozens of motivated entrepreneurs to identify their unique advantages in the marketplace and create a plan for increased productivity and business success.

With a knack for asking the right questions, real-life training and experience as a serial entrepreneur, and a hard-earned MBA, I'm equipped to help you overcome the roadblocks that are in the way of you running a profitable business.

Armed with a proven methodology, a safe and welcoming coaching style, and a genuine desire to see you win, I'm here for you.

To access my resource library, click the link below to gain tools to help you achieve your business goals at bit.ly/infocusresources

Interested in working with me? Schedule a 30-minute discovery call at bit.ly/rp30minchatchew

Application:

1. Complete the Brand Identity Worksheet
2. Complete the Brand Descriptives Worksheet
3. Complete the Brand Colors Worksheet
4. Download the Photoshoot checklist
5. If you are seeking help with any of these areas of your business or want to connect to a thriving business coaching community to grow as an

entrepreneur, schedule a 30-minute discovery call at
bit.ly/rp30minchatchew

PART II
PRIORITY

CHAPTER 11

THE 5 BIGGEST LIES OF PRODUCTIVITY

I t's one thing to know who you are, who you serve, what unique solution you provide, and the promised outcome you deliver. Now it's about prioritizing the highest leveraging actions to help you produce the outcome you seek. However, before we look at how to prioritize your business actions effectively, we have to change your paradigm for productivity, which are learned norms in our societal structure. In this chapter, I will cover the 5 biggest lies of productivity people believe. I will dispel these lies once and for all! These lies need to be dispelled so you can eliminate the feeling of being stuck and gain proven methodology to get things done in route to growing your business.

Lie #1: Everything matters equally.

"The things that matter most must never be at the mercy of things which matter least." - Joanne Wolfgang.

When I hear this quote, the first thing that comes to mind is the Five Love Languages by Gary Chapman. This concept says that there are five different love languages, and we each have a different love language as our top one. Acts of service, physical touch, quality time, receiving gifts, and words of affirmation are the five love languages.

My wife's top two are acts of service and quality time. Knowing that, suppose I came home every day with a gift, or I came home every day and just gave her words of affirmation. If I put a lot of effort into physical touch and was really affectionate, but I wasn't giving her quality time, and I wasn't doing things for her, would she be happy with me?

Here's the reality. I might be working really hard in the relationship, and she could not be happy because I'm not doing the things that matter most to her. How most people love is just an example of what is important to them. In their mind, they are making the largest deposits with this individual. If I spent time with my wife and I did things for her, but not the other things, she would feel loved by me because I'd be spending time on the actions that make the biggest deposits.

Even if I put in more time doing those other things, I wouldn't be making massive love deposits needed for us to have a successful relationship. And so it is with entrepreneurial productivity. We can do things in our day that will have a more significant effect on our ability to accomplish our goals than others. Our ability to identify and complete our most important work versus doing busy work will determine our ultimate results.

Lie #2. Multitasking is good.

In corporate America, if you can juggle multiple things at a time, that's a good thing. As a matter of fact, it is a badge of honor.

Well, I'm here to tell you, not only is it not good, it's not even a real thing.

"To do two things is to do neither." -Publilius Cyrus

I think about being at work. I've had times where I've written an email, and I get to a point where I'm replying to the email, and something or someone else grabs my attention. Then, I'm called off to that particular thing. I eventually come back to the office. I get back to my desk, and I go to my email again. Unfortunately, I have to go back to the beginning of the email that was written to me to read the context of the email and discover where I was in my response, and maybe I need to start completely over.

Maybe what I wrote initially doesn't even make sense to me with where my mind was at that time, or I have to go back to the beginning to figure things out. If I had just stayed at my desk and finished the email, that would be done in way less time. And my mind would be free to give my next task my undivided attention.

Here's the reality researchers have found. 27% of productivity is a loss every day by multitasking. We are actually losing when we engage in the habit of going from one thing to another without finishing one first. When you finish one task, you close that door in your mind to that task, and you have more mental space freed up to focus intensely on what you're doing at that moment.

When you "multitask," what you're really doing is task switching. Your conscious mind can only focus on one thing at a time. This is the part of your brain used to complete a fresh task for which you must concentrate. It's impossible for it to focus on two things at once.

Some things do not require conscious thought, like commuting to work with which we can do something else while we do things like listening to an audiobook in the car. You don't need to think about the directions or where you need to turn; it just kind of naturally happens. However, there are things as it relates to productivity that require our conscious mind. Have you ever been in a conversation, and someone's been talking to you, and you say, "Wait, what did you say again?"

The reason you have to do that is that you're replying to a social media post, replying to an email, or doing something else on your phone. Therefore, the person has to go back and repeat themselves again and again. Unfortunately, your phone tasks and your conversation is not getting your optimal attention. If you're trying to focus on what a person is saying while you're replying to a message, a good thing people say is, "Hey, give me one second. I just have to finish replying to this, and I'll be right with you." You have to close one door before you can open another successfully.

Lie # 3: Balance is a worthy aim.

To achieve extraordinary results, you must choose what matters most and give it all the time it demands. You actually must be out of balance in relation to all other work issues. This was one thing that was very clear to me when I wrote my first book a few years ago. I was on an ambitious timeline in writing the book because I wanted to help many students and colleagues who were led to talk to me about faith over the years with a practical guide on building their faith life.

I felt like I could never finish a conversation with those I spoke to about spiritual development because there were always more elements I needed to complete the puzzle. Therefore, I needed to write the book.

Once I finally sat down and decided to write the book, my wife was pregnant; we had just gotten married earlier that year, in May of 2015. My son was set to be born in January of 2016. Instinctively, I knew my son was coming, and I had to get this book done before he arrived. I knew I couldn't have my wife say, "Hey babe, I'm over here," and I reply with, "I'm writing my book, but I'll be right with you when our son wakes up in the middle of the night!"

It was September. My son was due in January. I had three months to write like a mad man. I realized the further I get away from a goal that I set for myself, the less likely it is to happen. Once I recognized that, I put my head down and completed the book.

While working full time and caring for my wife, who was preparing to have our first child, I just locked in. I was waking up really early. I was going to bed really late writing this, and I wasn't sleeping much. I just had a laser-like focus on finishing the book. During this time, I violated my sleep principles. Ideally, I like to get at least five to six hours of sleep. However, I wasn't getting six hours during these three months. I was staying up late, waking up early, knocking it out. But when it was done, it was done and out of my queue.

Then, I could be fully present when my son was born. He had me waking up in the middle of the night, changing him, feeding him, consoling him, or whatever was needed. I could be totally present for my wife at that time, while others could finish our past spiritual conversations by reading the book. It was a win-win for my family and those I was seeking to serve!

All this to say, to accomplish things, you have to get out of balance. Know that it is indeed normal to achieve extraordinary results. Know that when you lock in on something, sometimes you might forget to eat, you might sacrifice sleep, you just do certain things that you wouldn't normally do for the sake of the result.

When Olympians are preparing for the Olympics, they practice way out of proportion to how they might normally practice to accomplish such a tremendous feat of winning an Olympic medal.

What we should do is not balance but counterbalance. We should give an area of our lives the attention it needs for the moment until it no longer needs that level of focus or dedication. However, we must recognize the balls we juggle are made of different materials.

As Gary Keller puts it in The One Thing, "There's some balls that are made of rubber and there are other balls that are made of glass. You have to determine what balls are made of rubber and what balls are made of glass in your life. Usually, with work balls and social balls if we drop those a little bit, they'll bounce back for us." That's what happened to me in the case of writing the book.

I wasn't going above and beyond at work, and my socializing was really cut. I was giving work the time it needed, but nothing more so I could finish the book. The ball that is made of glass is typically the family ball. If I sit my wife up on a shelf for a year and I say, Hey, I'm working on this project for a year. I'll be back to get you next year. It's not going to work out too well. My wife would most likely want to leave me if I went that route.

You have to determine for yourself which balls are made of glass and which balls are made of rubber for you. Recognize that if you drop a ball made of glass, it'll be severely damaged, shattered, or lost. You must know how far that is acceptable for you to bend the pendulum as you navigate through your goals. But don't feel bad if you need to dedicate a disproportionate amount of time on something for some time because it is required for extraordinary results. Otherwise, you will have to be satisfied with ordinary results.

Lie #4: Successful people are unicorns.

This is simply a lie. They weren't born with these superhuman traits. They aren't impossible people. Trust me. I know it can certainly feel like this as we admire certain people and what they've been able to accomplish. We may find ourselves saying things like, "I wish I were born with those traits that they have." But the reality is that you build one habit at a time. Success is sequential, not simultaneous. So many times, we're trying to eat the elephant in one bite. And that's why we feel less than. Therefore, we don't attempt to eat some elephants because we decide we can't eat it in one bite.

I've talked to people in the past who were trying to stop smoking. They've said when they drink, they are more likely to smoke. They've said when they eventually quit; it was because they stopped drinking first. That first step led to them not having as much temptation where they wanted to smoke. Also, not drinking no longer made it fun to be in certain environments where they were likely to smoke. They were able to cut that habit out of their life completely.

When I think about a comparable habit in my own life, I think of eating healthy. When I exercise, eating healthy comes naturally to me. I feel like I don't want to mess up the workout by eating trash. In my mind, those things go together. Vice versa, when I'm not exercising, I'm feeling more stagnant, feeling lazier. I'm more likely to eat trash because my motivation is gone. This leads me to carelessness like drinking a lot of soda and the artificial energy that comes with it instead of producing the natural energy from my body through physical activity. But the point that I'm making is that you build habits one at a time.

I think about when I wanted to solve a Rubik's cube. When I had this on my mind as a goal, it seemed impossible. Honestly, I would look at the cube and say there's no way; only geniuses can do Rubik's Cubes. I marveled at this feat until one day, I said to myself, I wonder if people online are talking about doing this. So I pulled up some videos and pdf lessons on how to solve the Rubik's Cube.

Once I saw where it was explained, I said to myself, "there's a formula." Therefore, I learned that formula to solve it. I learned to do the top, then the middle, then the bottom. Once I learned this, I felt like a unicorn, even though my IQ did not raise any points. I simply knew the formula.

I said to myself, this is not about being a genius. This is about knowing the formula. So that's what I want to tell you. Success is just really about knowing the formula. I'm giving you the formula right now to dispel these lies that you can eliminate to increase your productivity and business. Successful people are not unicorns. They just built one habit at a time. So that's where you can start.

Lie #5: Big is bad.

You may have a friend who says, "I'm not negative; I'm realistic." I have plenty of people in my life like this. They often refer to what's realistic but do not aim high. Here's the reality. We are kept from our goal, not by obstacles, but by a clear path to a lesser goal. If we don't think big, we don't get really serious about going after what's truly on our hearts. All that's going to occupy our time is a clear path to lesser stuff.

I think about Walt Disney as it relates to this particular concept. I think about how we all marvel at the Disney conglomerate now, but this plan was all mapped out by Walt Disney. This guy had gone bankrupt nine different times! He had several bumps along the way of building his empire. However, if he hadn't mapped out Disney world and had a clear vision for what he wanted in the future, there is no way he would have been able to fight through as many challenges as he did to bring it to fruition.

Today, very few people walk the face of the earth who would say they know nothing of the Disney empire. They've likely been impacted by Disney in some way, whether it'd be the movies, the parks, or the products. Disney began with the end in mind. He thought about his someday goal. Twenty years from now, what movement or empire would you like to create? When you get really clear about the future, what you need to do today becomes crystal clear.

The fact is, we dramatically underestimate what we can do in the long term, but then we dramatically overestimate what we can do in the short term. For instance, we might set a really large goal for this year. Because the goal is so large and unrealistic to where we are, we get discouraged, and we don't do much towards it.

However, we severely underestimate where we could be if we started at a practical place, a goal that we could reach right now in the short term, and then build on that momentum to carry us to this much larger goal. Not only is big not bad, but it's also actually necessary to map out a path to extraordinary results.

Application

1. How can you better differentiate the level of importance of each task on your daily task list? How can this one change improve your level of productivity?
2. What triggers can you insert in your life to stop multitasking on conscious brain activities?
3. How has a constant focus on balance hindered you from your ability to achieve your business goals in the past?
4. What habit can you implement right away that would have the greatest impact on your ability to reach your most important business goal?
5. What is the most audacious business goal you have for 20+ years from now? Think big!

CHAPTER 12

THE SIMPLE PATH TO PRODUCTIVITY

———o———

"Success is simple. Do what's right the right
way at the right time." -Arnold Iasso.

It's funny because we have these big rocks in life, and we have small rocks that create a hard choice. Should we complete the big rocks first, or the small rocks? The big rocks are major projects that will move the needle most in our lives, while the small rocks are considered low hanging fruit. I consider things like washing the dishes, doing the laundry, folding clothes as low hanging fruit. Although these items may not move the needle in our worlds, they can usually get done quicker and often provide enough distraction to block us from our larger projects.

If most of our attention goes towards these small rocks, we eventually have no room for the big rocks in our lives. However, if we put the big rocks first, we'll have room to throw the other little rocks. This concept is demonstrated beautifully through a rock video I saw a long time ago that visually represents the rock concept. Check out this rock video at bit.ly/infocusbookrocks. It's about seven minutes long and helps to truly give you a deeper understanding of the concept.

Another scenario to help visualize this concept is one my grandfather organized every time we went on a long trip. He would always say, before packing the car, "Give me the biggest luggage first."

I realized that if we put the big items first, we'll be able to maneuver the other little bags just to fit in around and in the corners of the trunk. Whereas, if we put the little bags first, there will be no room for the big bags. He was teaching me this at a very young age, but I never equated it to productivity. However, it absolutely highlights this major productivity principle I want to share with you.

Before we go forward, we have to start with this focusing question before asking what type of rock a task or project falls into. The focusing question is, what is the one thing I can do such that I will make everything else easier or unnecessary by doing it?

The successful mindset says until my one thing is done, everything else is a distraction. It's really hard to think of things this way because things always come up. People always ask for help. People always want to have conversations. When we live our lives in the truth that before I put this big bag in my trunk, I cannot do any of the above, we won't achieve extraordinary results. It sounds harsh because it requires you to tell people no at times, but it's required to build something noteworthy. When it comes to productivity, I talked about three buckets at the very beginning of the book. We've already addressed the purpose bucket. In this section, we address the priority bucket.

Purpose really is your big one thing. It's what you were created for. My big one thing is to thrust people into action through practical solutions and a unique perspective. That will take on many shapes, sizes, and roles throughout my life. However, it's the one thing I should never neglect to do. That's the big one thing. That is the thing that guides the rest of the ship. And that's why we started with purpose before we moved on to any of the other buckets. Now you are ready to deal with the priority bucket.

Let's think about using a screwdriver. We can use a screwdriver to do one or two things—to screw a screw in and out of a wall, a frame, or whatever a screw goes into. However, I've seen people successfully use the back of it as well. They use it as a hammer to hit a nail into something.

That's a great use for a screwdriver, but it's not the optimal use. The optimal use for why the screwdriver was created was to screw things in and out of wherever they go. The point of thinking about using the screwdriver is to realize that you might be experiencing success in an area, but I want you to question, is this what you were created to do?

When we start to think about a thing's purpose, we become interested in its optimal use. We know that even if you're successfully banging things with the back of the screwdriver, there's another level that you have to go. This is why defining this purpose bucket is so important that you can move from good, to great, to phenomenal.

Years ago, I invested in a real estate coaching program with a strategy was to use real estate to fund my dreams and my ability to do other things. What I soon realized was my personality type was not cut out for the real estate game. Especially not for it to be my primary focus.

Don't hear what I'm not saying. I'll still invest in real estate in the future. I also think everyone should invest in real estate because we already are if we are renting a place or buying a place. Although I'm not talking down on real estate, still you have to devote time to anything you do well. The time I spent chasing real estate caused me to neglect my one thing. Don't get it twisted; if you want to be successful in real estate, you need one of two things—money or investing a lot of time. There's no in-between. Either you need money, or you need time. So what I realized, based on neglecting my one thing to go after real estate, was that what I was doing was suppressing my ability to make more money I could invest in real estate in the future.

It's your gift that makes room for you. Once you can show the world that this is me, this is my value, this is what I bring to the marketplace; then, the marketplace pays you back. But if you don't show the marketplace what you're worthy of, then you just have to fight through, never quite breaking through that glass ceiling cycle.

That's what I was doing. It got me to a really dark place because I felt like I wasn't flying, but I quickly recommitted to my purpose. Now, I feel there's no way I can never be totally locked into my purpose, and it be my priority.

Your purpose is the straightest path to extraordinary results. After struggling with real estate for almost a year, I realized the money I earned from my courses, coaching, and other services brought me the money I needed to invest in real estate faster. This way, I could take advantage of the real estate stability, predictability, financial strength without taking away time from growing my purpose movement. Always remember, nobody can beat you at being you when you are you, and you're in the right market that will pay you.

If you still have questions about your gift or market, let's connect in a 30-minute chat and chew at Bit.ly/rp30minchatchew. What if this is the call you need to gain the clarity necessary for you to get unstuck?

Alright, let's get back to business. The bucket we're in right now is the priority bucket. This is your small one thing. Your small one thing consists of your short term goals down to what you should be focused on today. You may know your gift, but purpose without priority is powerless. Hence, the following chapters will help you set up your priorities and bring extreme clarity and mobility to your purpose. This concept is all about lining up your route.

The pace bucket is all about managing and increasing your productive energy while on the right route. Within energy management, you have spiritual energy. For me, this energy is a source of life and strength I need to make a meaningful impact, not a surface-level impact. When I meditate, I think about my relationship with God and what that means for how I should live today. Not only today, but also the direction I'm going in the future. It really paints my outlook. Although there's no hard and fast rule as to where you should start, I like to start there. Once my spiritual energy is lined up, I'm able to place everything happening that day and that season in its rightful place.

Then there's physical energy. Sleep, diet, and exercise are the major elements that impact your physical energy. When I'm getting the right amount of sleep, sleeping at the right time, sleeping in the right way, I'm giving my body the real food it needs to thrive, and I'm exercising to get myself in a peak state; I'm in the position to follow through on my mission with reckless abandon.

Another element of energy management is emotional energy. For this area, I do a gratitude practice where, at the beginning of my day, I ask myself, what am I most grateful for? What about that makes me grateful? How does that make me feel? Think about this in your life right now. I sometimes take it a step further and go to the last 24 hours. Sometimes when you don't put that time constraint on it, you end up coming up with similar stuff every day, and your practice can get stale. I like looking at gratitude in the context of the last 24 hours because it keeps me alive to every day.

Then there's mental energy. This energy sparks the goals you have through the plans you develop from your calendar activities, the books you read, audiobooks you listen to, podcasts you listen to, and like-minded communities you join.

This paints your world and creates a strong mind to really follow your gift. Those are all the buckets that help you make your business pop.

We're going to look at the priority bucket in this section of the book. I just wanted to paint that entire picture so you can see the strategic order in establishing your purpose, lining things up the way they should be lined up, and managing your energy to accelerate your growth. That's the simple path to extraordinary results.

A couple of books that really dig into this subject, even more, are the ONE Thing by Gary Keller and Eat that Frog by Brian Tracy. Also, be sure to check out the rock video at bit.ly/infocusbookrocks.

Application

1. Check out the rock video at bit.ly/infocusbookrocks
2. What is one thing you can do at night and/or in the mornings to better prioritize your daily activities based on the productivity pathway shared in this chapter?

CHAPTER 13

APPLIED KNOWLEDGE IS POWER

―――――o―――――

"Theory without practice is useless, and practice without theory is dangerous." - Emmanuel Kahn.

With all the knowledge you've learned in this book so far, you will remain out of alignment without a strategic way to execute it.

In the past, when I did something as simple as writing out my to-do list, I was checking things off and moving through things quickly. I felt like a boss. I was knocking down my list. However, I didn't have a strategic plan to accelerate my results. It was just writing things down and getting things done, but I wasn't even in the first gear of productivity with this strategy. I was all over the place, and I didn't have any boundaries.

I didn't have anything to constrict me so that I could explode my results. I wasn't operating off the principle that I previously talked to you about with my grandfather who said,

"Put the biggest luggage first." I was just checking things off the list. I ended up exhausted and disappointed with no system.

In the end, I had many goals, checking things off, but not really building a high level of consistency because I wasn't smart about my goals. I had no real plan.

Let me talk you through a strategic plan I've learned using this concept. It's called SMART goals. The S in SMART goals stands for specific. You have to specify the amount of money you want to make; you can't just say I want to make a lot of money. The amount of money you want to earn starts to paint the picture of how much work you will have to produce. That's why it's so important. Next, it needs to be measurable. It needs to be specific and measurable, so you know if you hit it. What you cannot measure, you cannot improve.

Next, your goals need to be attainable. Is it something that's in your power? Remember, we drastically overestimate what we can do in the short term. Is it attainable based on where you are as far as your experience and level of education? Is it attainable? Is it realistic based on what your past performance has been in the previous year or month? Are you trying to go from zero to a hundred thousand in a year? That's great in theory, but if you never made 20,000, why don't we start there? Because even if you exceed 20,000, you will still have accomplished your goal.

Next, is your goal relevant? Is this even something you will be satisfied with once you get the outcome? Will it bring you closer to your future goals? If not, let's not waste time going in that direction. Finally, is your goal time-bound? When are you going to do this? What date are you going to set? Those are the smart components.

I believe in really shooting for the moon; however, if you bring your goals close enough to you, you are more likely to put in the work to accomplish it in the short term.

Big is not bad. However, without your goals being smart, it's not very likely that you're going to achieve them. If you have a system that's working for you, stick to it. I mean that sincerely. I remember I had a great jump shot in high school. Then I got a personal coach who changed my shot. It ruined my consistency as a shooter, and I'm still a little salty about it. Therefore, if your current goal-setting strategy is working for you, then stick with it. I just wanted to bring this to you because it's been my experience that you might be banging on some nails with the back of the screwdriver, but if you flip the screwdriver around, it could work better for you.

In conclusion, if a goal is close enough to you, you're going to work harder to reach it. On the other hand, if it's too far, you'll quit in discouragement. For instance, if I was doing 49 pushups and 55 was right there, I would probably struggle to do the other six. But if my goal was a hundred and I was at 49, I'm stopping at 49. 100 is just too far. The psychology of that is demotivating. I don't want you not just to have goals, but smart goals.

Application:

1. What are your three most important business goals right now? Ask yourself and answer this question within 30 seconds. You can flesh the goals out as the timer expires to ensure the goals include all of the SMART Goal elements. However, we tend to write what we truly want when we don't give ourselves too much time to talk our way out of them. These answers will tell you what is really important to you.

CHAPTER 14

BIGGER IS BETTER

"Our problem is not that we aim too high and miss,
but that we aim too low and hit." - Les Brown

L et's talk about this concept called goal setting to the now. This concept is really the reverse of how we typically set our goals. We typically look at goals from a one-year, three-year, and even five-year increments. I want to encourage you to look even further out and work your way back to the most relevant action you can do at this moment. Let me set the scene up for you.

I want you to think in terms of what you want to leave on this earth. When people are at your memorial, what would you want them to know, do, or experience? What is it you want to leave? I want you to think that far out because something happens when we think that far out. That kind of thinking takes the limits off of our minds. It allows you to reach further than you ever thought you could. Before we go there, I want to show you the problem with thinking too short-term. Then, I'll go further out and show you the beauty of longer-term thinking.

The issue with thinking too short-term is the same issue with the US presidential office terms. The US presidents set goals in four-year increments because that's how long their presidential term lasts. The problem with this, is the US president is completing actions that will make them look best or make the country look best for those four years. They don't have a high motivation for twenty plus years or further out than this. Their decisions are made today that may be positive for today, but not years and years down the road.

They may make a decision that could be terrible for the country long-term. However, we are not necessarily set up best as a country long-term because of this restriction. And worse, we are looking at our lives the same way. We're looking at our lives in one year, three to five-year segments. I've even heard of people looking at their lives no further out than a quarter. If we only look at life in these short terms, the goal that we achieve may not stack up to where we ultimately want to go. This kind of thing does not happen organically. You must be intentional.

Positive things do happen while going in a positive direction, but those positive things may not be optimal for your direction. You can gain a lot of progress in one area, switch your direction, and then go on to another area because you're just thinking short-term all the time. However, when you think about someday from now, what it can look like, it can look like Disney.

When Walt Disney envisioned Disney World, he was thinking twenty plus years ahead. This imagination carried him to Disney World, which we experience now. It's beyond what most people could think imagine. But I want you to challenge yourself. If you would dare to think about the long-term and work our way back to today, you could create something unforgettable!

With that knowledge, I want you to revisit your five-year vision if you've completed the brand vision worksheet at bit.ly/infocusbooksresources. When writing the vision, I want you to think about this focusing question. What is the one thing you can leave on earth that would make anything else you want easier or unnecessary?

A supporting thought to processing this question is coming with an answer to this question in the three most important areas of your life. Develop a one-sentence goal for each of those areas, with what you want to leave someday from now. Within that, think about the one thing out of those three goals that would make the other two easier or unnecessary. You even want to prioritize those goals because we need to have one major focus?

Think about this. If you want to be 'here' twenty plus years from now, 'here's' where you need to be in five years. If I want to be a billionaire twenty plus years from now, 'here's' where you need to be in five years to be on pace for that. What's the one thing you can do in the next five years that will have you on pace for your twenty-year goal?

Then we break it down even further. What's the one thing you can do in the next year to be on pace for where you want to be five years from now. And then we go further, what's the one thing you can do in this quarter to put you on pace for your year goal. What's the one thing you can do this month to be on pace for your quarter goal. What's the one thing you can accomplish this week to be on pace for where you want to be a month from now? What the one thing you can do today to be in pace for your weekly goal? Finally, what's the one thing you can do right now to be on pace to hit today's goal?

This is how you move from theory to practice. This is not just a pie in the sky idea without taking this strategic action in the priority bucket. Two worksheets accompany this exercise called Goal Setting to the Now and the Weekly Focus Plan at bit.ly/infocusbookresources. You will need to designate a championship goal for the three major areas in your life. My three areas are faith, family, and finances. Once you're finished completing your twenty-year pathway, you are ready to complete your weekly focus plan and look at this document every single day.

This sheet is going to guide your focus every week. Indicate your championship goal for each area at the top of the sheet and break each section down. So when you look at your year, you can see your annual goals, quarterly goals, monthly goals, and your weekly goals all in one place. On the back of the sheet, you'll see that there's a 80% tasks. The 20% big rocks that go on the front of the sheet and the 80% tasks go on and back. This is called the 80/20 rule based on Pareto's Principle, which says that 20% of the work you do gives you 80% of your results. If that's the case, your weekly focus plan only has 20% of the most needle-moving action items that give you 80% of your results upfront. The 80% small tasks that only give us 20% of our results go on the back.

This sheet is most effective if you promise not to flip to the back of the page until your front page is complete. Remember, the front page action items are the big rock activities. These are the things that are going to warrant the biggest results. If you get those done, you earn the right to move to the back of the sheet to complete the rest of your tasks.

Set aside some time right now to determine when you're going to complete your weekly focus plan each week. I promise you, if you only focus on your lead domino until it's complete, everything else will be easier or unnecessary for you.

Application

1. Revisit your Brand Vision Worksheet
2. Complete Your Goal Setting to the Now Worksheet
3. Complete Your Weekly Focus Plan

CHAPTER 15

THE IMPORTANCE OF VISION

"You must begin with the end in mind." - Stephen Covey

Some people just start with an idea they can make money with. They end up changing lanes and businesses all together because of a lack of vision. It's almost like a hoarder who has so many things because they attract different visions that they act on frequently, but do not have one clear direction. That's why for many of us, entering the home of a hoarder makes us feel like we can't think. Sadly, many serial entrepreneurs have brains that look like this and are stuck because of it. They have so much stuff in their brains; they don't know what to do with it all. The Bible says where there is no vision, people perish. The way I've seen this play out in business is where there is no vision, the business doesn't survive. It typically goes away most likely because the entrepreneur did not strategize about where they were going.

Here's a quick story about something I did to illustrate this example. Years ago, I started this thing called daily entrepreneurial reflections on Facebook Live at 7 a.m. I realized I did not know where I wanted to take my audience or where I wanted to go with it, so I shut it down. It was funny because I actually got people who were interested in the beginning. They were excited about it. They would look forward to seeing it every morning, but it really lost steam when I didn't know where I wanted to go. Although my gift was being used through this experience, I started seeing that I needed to be clear about exactly where I wanted to go and where I would take my people.

As it turned out, I was in the right lane but just didn't have a plan. I didn't map it out. As evidenced by this book being read by you, all my hard work didn't go to waste. Sometimes when you're starting out in business, you don't understand a lot and have to figure things out. However, I don't recommend just starting without a plan.

What happens, is you get much further along faster if you start with a plan than if you just start mindlessly doing stuff. One thing that can't be understated is I had to take a step away from these videos so that when I launched my brand for the way I wanted people to see me, they could see what I wanted them to see.

Here's my suggestion. We're putting this puzzle together for your business, so instead of just randomly having the pieces and trying to figure things out, my suggestion is let's look at the box. If we look at the box, you can determine what it's supposed to look like in the end. If you can determine what it's supposed to look like in the end, that informs your actions right now. This is a good time to review your brand vision worksheet and your weekly focused plan to help you identify exactly where you want to go. Once you know what your vision is, only then can you begin working towards it.

In the next chapter, we're going to move beyond your business's skeleton and onto the meat and bones by examining how to design the perfect business model for your business.

Application:

1. Review Your Brand Vision Worksheet
2. Review Your Weekly Focus Plan

CHAPTER 16

IDENTIFYING YOUR BUSINESS LEVELS

The great American philosopher, Meek Mill, said it best, "It's levels to this." When I say it's levels to this, I'm saying it's levels to people's relationship with your business. People typically don't meet you today and go in for the full meal deal tomorrow.

There are all sorts of avenues to try things out. Therefore, I think about my own consuming experience. I want you to think about your own consumer experience, how you move into people's business, how you are on boarded, or acclimated to the different companies you buy from.

I think about my experience with a professional development online community called Breathe University, where I connected with personal development guru Eric Thomas. I came across Breathe University by listening to free content on YouTube, from which came my initial introduction to Eric Thomas.

Then I started listening to the podcast, more free content! Yay! I listened to the podcast for about a year on my personal development journey. I kept hearing that people were doing really well for themselves as entrepreneurs in Breathe University.

There's a community of people doing all these amazing things. After hearing that for a year, I finally invested in Breathe University. It was the biggest investment I ever made for personal development, but I got more than I could ever ask for in return. I received courses, coaching, and a community to hold me accountable for what I said I would do. Since investing in Breathe University initially, I've paid for conferences, certifications, and additional coaching.

I've done that, but I didn't start out doing things like certifications immediately after jumping in. That all came later, but it certainly wasn't where I began. I needed to build trust with the business and the people I was doing business with. As it relates to your business, you must create those levels.

You must create those tiers for people to get the opportunity to taste test what you do. Think about Costco. They have many sample stations throughout the store. Some people go there just for the samples. They want you to taste a little bit of it.

You don't have to pay for it. They're giving it to you in hopes that you're going to open up and go ahead and take down a whole full meal deal because of the taste that you got at that moment that you enjoyed it. Even mall restaurants do this. That's what you need to set up for your business.

However, buying one meal isn't really becoming a loyal customer. That's a one-time deal. If I go beyond that and become a regular every time I come to the mall, that's the next level where you want to get your people to.

Go to bit.ly/infocusbookresources to access the business model worksheets. It will help you build the business model that's right for you. This pyramid you see pictured in **figure 16.1** is your business model roadmap. This information is at the bottom of your pyramid because it's your foundation for attracting people to you.

Figure 16.1

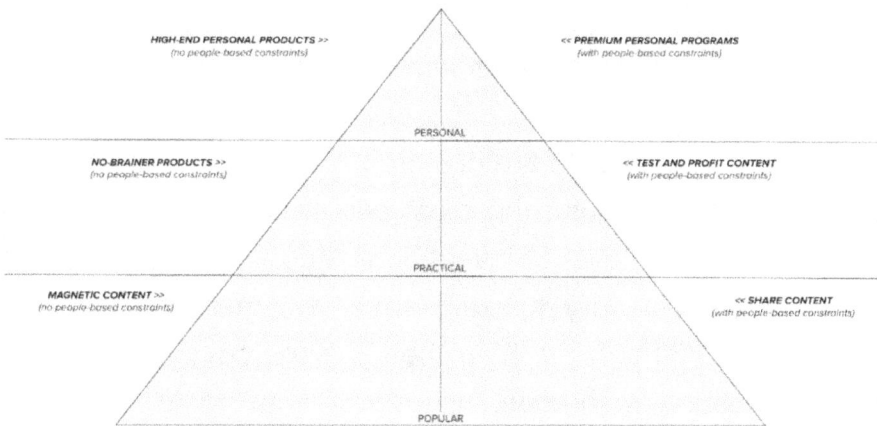

The worksheet covers all you need to know. You have access to a list of product ideas to build out your business pyramid in the book resources found at bit.ly/infocusbookresources. For example, my free level would be my eBook, resource library, podcast, video content, and audio content on social media and things of that nature. After the free level, you work your way up to the mid-level. Every business is not the same. So I want you to think about this as it relates to your business.

I want you to get your juices flowing into what you are going to provide for your customers. Then, move on up to designing your mid to high ticket offers. Mid-level offers can range from about $50 to a couple of hundred dollars, where I offer group coaching and courses.

Your mid-level high ticket item can be over a longer time typically, or a lot more value is packed inside it. And then, there is your flagship offer.

This is not necessarily what most people will do, but you're going to get a few people who will do this and pretty much equal what most people are doing on the lower levels. The top-level people will require the most personal time and attention just based on the level of investment. You will be able to flush this out and get very specific once you start the business model worksheets in the resource library at bit.ly/infocusbookresources. Here's an example below in **figure 16.2**.

Figure 16.2

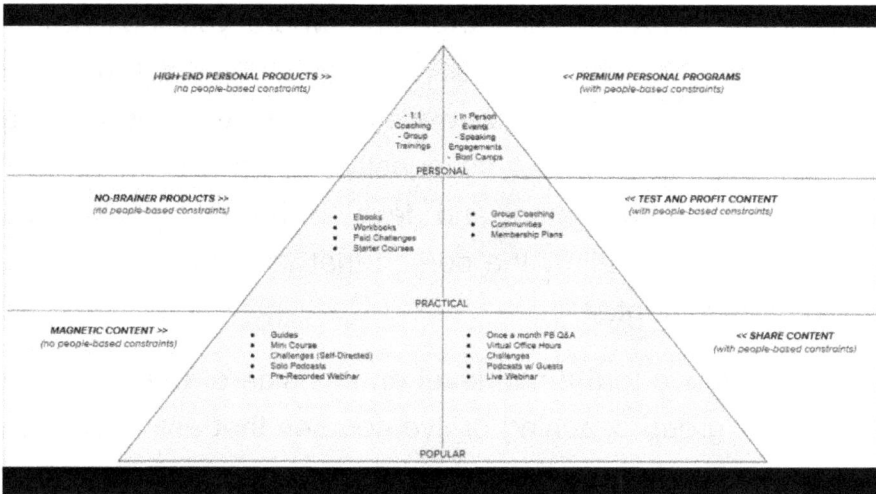

You're going to fill this out for yourself. You will see it broken down in a way where on one side, you have no people-based constraints, and on the other side, you have people-based constraints. For instance, no people-based constraints at that magnet low level would be a solo podcast. You don't need another person to record it. However, there are time-based constraints because you have to create the content on your own. You won't be asking anybody questions, so you have to deliver for that time period.

Then you have no brainer products like an ebook or a free guide, where there's still no people constraints because you can write on your own. On the mid-level, you may put together a really good course that helps someone solve a problem without wasting more time, energy, or money. Your high-end personal product is where you are the only one that needs to be there, maybe one-on-one coaching. This offer doesn't require anyone else to be there other than you and the client.

Then you move to the other side where you look at low-level items with people-based constraints but not have as many time constraints. If you were to interview someone, that wouldn't have as many time constraints because you don't have to create the content and develop the content. You just ask questions and allow the person that you're interviewing to provide the content.

As you move to the mid-level on this side of the chart, you might offer group coaching or live courses that are dependent on people showing up. If you record the course, people can go through the information at their leisure. However, if you set things up for people to do together, they are going to have to show up for it to be considered group coaching. If only have a couple of people show up to be coached, it may not feel right for people, and your business reputation could suffer because of it. That's the second tier.

Then there are the high-tier offers on the people-based constraints side—here's where you would do things like live events. Live events definitely have people-based constraints as you're the one who has to recruit the people for the event, coordinate speaker schedules, and things of that nature. Those are three different tiers.

So let's review what I just discussed. For example, you can look at me doing the course version of this book. This had time constraints for it. I had to sit down and do the course. It took me time to write the outline. It took me time to create the slide deck. It took me time to record the audio. It had time constraints, but no people based constraints. I set it up myself and did it. Please go to bit.ly/infocusbookresources to review the products and content to fill your product pyramid list. On one side of the chart, you will see items with time constraints, but no people-based constraints. You will see items with people-based constraints on the other side of the chart, but not time-constraints. It is more of an exhaustive list than the items we covered in this chapter on each pyramid level.

3 things that your perfect business model is based on.

#1: Your current income. Your current income, your savings, the money that you have is investment power. To grow a business, one of your greatest assets is your income from your current job. If you have money, the business model that makes sense for you would look a lot different than the person who has no money to invest. In business, your financial investment level is referred to as the amount of skin you have in the game.

If you don't have much income now, no worries. You can use your income to do something like a course. I run courses, paid a small membership for the course platform, and opened money-making opportunities through my online course for a fee as low as $39 a month for the course platform. Starting in business, you most likely don't have a lot, so you do things that don't cost you a lot of money or very little. However, you could still offer a lot of value even if what you're producing has a low expense.

#2: Your time. What type of time do you have? Are you full time and you only have maybe an hour or two a day to work on your business? Are you part-time, and you have half the day to work on your business? Are you unemployed, and you have all day to work on your business? All of those factors are going to determine what type of business model is best suited for you? Building something takes a lot of your time and attention. Make sure your business model is realistic to the amount of time you have to serve people. If you put together a business model without enough time to execute it, you may get a bad name and be unable to continue your business forward because of the negativity surrounding your brand. You want to make sure that whatever you do is sustainable and fits your current lifestyle.

#3: Your experience. Based on your industry expertise, there may be certain relationships you can leverage that will work for you. If you have a whole lot of contacts in a particular arena and you wanted to create a mastermind community, you might be able to leverage your network to set this up.

You want to evaluate these three things for you. What do you have most of? Do you have more money, time, or experience? After you evaluate this, you want to plan and understand your business model based on those factors. Based on those factors, let's walk through it. What are the revenue sources that you can create? How much time do you have to create different revenue sources? What does that look like for you? I encourage you to look at the list and sift through what works for you.

To take things a step further, I want you to think about all the things you can do beyond the list. Don't just be restricted by that list as it's just to get you started.

The next thing you will want to think through is how you explain your product. Who does it help? What unique solution does it offer them? What is the transformation they will receive as a result? Who is your target market? Why are these people motivated to use your business? The motivation I'm thinking about is the way people feel about tissue paper. It is never going out of business because people are always going to have to use the bathroom. These people are very motivated to buy Scott or Angel Soft because they absolutely can't live without it. They're motivated. So you want to think about why your market is motivated to buy from you in these terms. Next, you want to consider your business expenses. What is it going to cost to produce your offer from start to finish? Like, what are all the things you must pay for to produce your product or service? What are your membership fees for different platforms, for your website, or anything else?

What are your profit margins? How much does it cost for you to make? It's important to know these numbers, so you are not doing things that don't make sense, like producing a product for $40 and charging $30 for it.

For instance, for me investing in my teachable platform to make sense, I need to have at least one person pay me $40 to break even. Then, anything I make above that will be a profit for me as far as courses are concerned.

Another thing to think about is lead generation. What are you doing to attract clients? What's your magnet, your sales process after a client says, "I'm interested. I want to do it"? What does that next step look like? Is that an easy onboarding type of a situation?

Then, how are you going to evaluate the customer experience? I know this is a lot to think about, but are necessary questions to build a successful business.

Download and complete all business model worksheets at bit.ly/infocusbookresources. I know if you're reading this book, you're serious about actually building a profitable business. I know you don't just want to say you're an entrepreneur, but actually that you run a business. Take action on the worksheets below asap!

Application:

1. Download and complete the Product Pyramid
2. Download the Products to Fill in Your Product Pyramid
3. Complete Questions to Help You Plan & Understand Your Business Model

CHAPTER 17

BUDGETING YOUR TIME

O nce your business model is planned out, you must have a solid execution plan. Planning the business model and coming up with ideas typically isn't what stops entrepreneurs from making one business pop. It is the management of an asset that you can neither produce nor get more of—TIME.

You may be thinking I don't have enough time, but I'm telling you to look again. I'm reminded of this story in the Bible, where the disciples, Peter and Andrew, were fishing all day and hadn't caught anything. This was their job. They were professional fishermen. I'm sure they were thinking, look we'd tried. We are about to shut it down. But Jesus comes out there, and he says, "Lower your net." Peter said, "we have been out here all day, but alright." Almost like when someone asks you to click a button on an electronic device, and you know it no longer works.

Nonetheless, they lowered their nets and brought back up so many fish the boat broke. This was a shocking situation; however, because the brothers, Peter and Andrew, came with open hearts to the situation, and they got blessed. I'm telling you right now; you have more time than you would believe. What is it going to take for you to realize it? It's going to take you going through the time-management activities in the resource library to understand. Many people understand this budgeting concept as it relates to money, but some of the same principles also work for budgeting your time.

We typically don't budget our time as intensely. We have meetings that we schedule, but it's just a whatever pop's up approach. It's just whatever our job uses our time for. If our boss schedules a meeting, we just attend without even thinking about it. I want you to take inventory of your time to begin gaining the type of control you need to build your business. Identify your time commitments. Download the 168-hour commitment worksheet & schedule worksheet at bit.ly/infocusbookresources.

When looking at your commitments and your schedule, I've found it best to look at this exercise through the lens of the 3 most important areas of my life. I use Faith (ministry), family (personal), and finances (business). Feel free to adjust the worksheet to fit your lifestyle. However, I do recommend limiting your sheet to 2 or 3 areas.

Your commitments and schedule exercises are where you go from saying a particular area of your life is important to it being planned, on your schedule, and actually important. Your schedule is where your priorities are set.

When completing the exercises, you must write out your commitments first, so your commitments inform your schedule, not the other way around. This way, you make sure your schedule is in alignment with who you want to become.

I want you to think about what's important to you and write a realistic time that you can dedicate to it. By realistic, if you have a full-time job where you work 40 hours, then you can't put less than 40 hours for work in your commitments. Also, include your commute in your work time.

You want to be realistic from the standpoint of all the big rocks that exist for you. The big rock areas that often are most predictable are your sleeping time, meal times, work hours, personal business hours, personal time, family time, and volunteer time. You can add any other thing that you want to add in there. Think about the time you need for your morning routine and other special commitments. Do not leave one second unaccounted for just like you would be encouraged not to leave one cent unaccounted for in your financial budget.

After completing this step, you will begin to chart your time on your schedule chart. Once you chart your time there, then you'll have a bird's eye view of your life weekly. It's here that you have the structure prepared to honor your one thing. At this point, it's about honoring what you put on paper. Here's a question you can ask yourself. If your one thing was on trial, would your calendar be able to convict it? If building your business is the lead domino to help you change the rest of your life, does your calendar reflect that? Is it prioritized on your calendar? To take it a step further, do you execute on your one thing before you do anything else? Are you following through?

I have a friend who told me something a long time ago that I'll never forget after a girl broke my heart. This girl would tell me she wanted to be with me but would always came up with excuses about why she couldn't be with me. Finally, one day my friend said, "You can't go by what people say. You have to go by what they do." That might seem simple to you, but that resonated deeply with me. So I'm saying that to you right now, I can't go by what you say is important; I have to go by what you actually do. You have to protect your time blocks at all costs because that's your future you're protecting.

You really have to take these activities seriously to finally build your business. Again, if your one thing was on trial, would your calendar be able to convict it? If your time blocking were on trial, would your calendar contain enough evidence to convict you?

It's going to take you some time to think through your commitments; however, your schedule will change at some point. Things are going to happen. There's going to be moving targets where you might have to adjust your schedule. So you shouldn't have the mindset of making your schedule and keeping the same one for all time's sake. Some adjustments will need to happen. However, always honor what you say you value. No one believes what you say, only what you do.

Application:

1. Complete The 168-Hour Commitments Worksheet
2. Complete The 168-Hour Schedule Chart

PART III
PACE

CHAPTER 18

ESTABLISHING YOUR MORNING ROUTINE

O ne of the things that help you to honor your time budget consistently is your habits and routines. It's not the big things you decide to do once in a blue moon that sets you up for success, but rather the things you repeatedly do on a daily basis.

"People don't decide their futures. They decide their habits and their habits decide their futures." - FM Alexander

I didn't really start to level up until I got my routines tight. The greatest example of the advantage of routines is a pro basketball player named Steph Curry.

I remember in 2016, he had one of the most unbelievable seasons ever in NBA history. He won the first-ever unanimous most valuable player award that season. One of the things I remember so vividly about that year is people would show up to watch Steph Curry's pregame routines.

As intriguing as the actual games were, Steph Curry would put so much time, effort, and energy into his pregame routine, fans found just as exciting to watch. It was as if he was floating on the court in his own world. When you get your routines in line, that's what life can feel like for you. It's almost like you have an unfair advantage. They give you control over your life.

I had a big challenge with just waking up when I wanted to years ago. At the beginning of that year, I remember the only goal I set for myself was to wake up every day at 5:30 a.m. That's the only goal I had because I recognized that if I could wake up on time, then the other things I wanted to do could not get done unless I woke up early enough.

A couple of months passed. However, this year was just like years past when I just fell off. I would wake up and hit the snooze button again and again until 7:30 a.m.

I needed help with this, so a friend suggested I read this book called the Miracle Morning by Hal Elrod. This book changed my life! It is on my Mount Rushmore of personal development books.

The most valuable thing I received from this book is the practical strategy Hal Elrod shared about overcoming the snooze button. This strategy has stood the test of times. It worked for me all those years ago, and it's still working for me today. This is what he suggested.

Step 1. Distance your phone/alarm across the room where you have to get out of bed and walk to it to turn the alarm off. Where I was living at the time, I could put my phone in the bathroom and keep my bathroom door open. So when my alarm went off in the morning, I would hear it in the bathroom, and I would have to walk to the bathroom to shut it off. The reason why that was significant is because of step two.

Step 2. Turn on the lights immediately. Nothing shocks your system like that bright light popping right on. After you've woken up and shut your alarm off, the lights come on.

Step 3. Drink a glass of water. When you're sleeping, your body becomes dehydrated. Drinking a glass or bottle of water automatically provides a level of oxygen and energy to your body. When you give yourself water, you are also giving your body an inner bath, cleansing it of toxins.

Step 4. Wash your face and brush your teeth. The water hitting your face provides another level of alertness, and fresh breath provides a fresh start to the day.

Step 5. Put on your exercise clothes immediately after coming out of the bathroom. Getting dressed and ready is really half the battle to start your day off feeling ready to go.

This formula literally took me from not being able to wake up on time every day to doing it consistently to the point where it's carried me to this point in my life. Although I'm not 100% perfect in this, I'm proud that I'm on top of this in my life.

After leaping over the huge hurdle of waking up when you want to, I want you to figure out your morning routine Mount Rushmore activity. What are the four things that you're going to commit to doing every morning faithfully? When waking up early, the temptation is to overload yourself with a whole bunch of expert morning routine ideas. I'm encouraging you to select 4 things you can stick with them just to get started. The four things on my Mount Rushmore are:

#1. Wake up when I get up. When I hear my alarm, I don't hit the snooze button. I get up and hit it and wake up.

#2. Quiet time with God. When I pour into my spiritual life, it spills over on everything else that I have to do and who I have to serve for the day.

#3. Education while exercising. I listen to audiobooks while riding my stationary bike. I take notes on my phone when I get to the good parts. I committed myself to take away at least one thing that I can apply immediately versus having this nervous energy about needing to get every point in the book or feeling like a failure. This strategy has accelerated my learning.

#4. Architecting my day. Every minute you spend in planning saves you ten minutes in execution. Thirty minutes of planning set me up for five clear and strong hours of productivity.

You will find the Morning Routine Mount Rushmore worksheet at bit.ly/infocusbookresources. On the worksheet, you will also find other morning routine honorable mentions.

Remember, people don't decide their futures; they decide their habits and their habits decide their futures. Therefore, commit to creating your Morning Routine Mount Rushmore.

Application:

1. Complete Morning Routine Mount Rushmore Worksheet

CHAPTER 19

ESTABLISHING YOUR EVENING ROUTINE

T he truth about a successful morning is that it starts the night before. One of the greatest examples that could explain this best is one night a friend invited me to a huge prize fight. There were going to be several men at the event I never met, and I really enjoy meeting new people. I was very excited. However, the next day I was tasked with a huge training assignment in a new leadership role at my church. I knew I needed to be on point.

I knew deep down if I went to the fight party, I would not be on point the following day for my leadership assignment. The fight didn't come on until almost midnight. Therefore, I decided not to attend the fight.

The next day I ended up having one of the best training sessions I've ever had in my life. I ended up performing at a really high level, and I would be a fool to believe that deciding to go home and go to bed early was unrelated to the success I experienced the next day.

It's not unrelated. You cannot stay up to two or three o'clock in the morning and expect to be operating at a peak level with peak energy the next day. I'm not saying that there aren't some unicorns out there who can do it. Unless you're one of those people, I suggest getting the amount of sleep you need at night before waking up in the morning.

I suggest establishing a bedtime routine. In the previous chapter, we talked about wake-up time. I had a goal of waking up at 5:30 a.m. daily. I wake up much earlier than that now, but I want you to establish your start time. Let's pretend five o'clock is going to be your start time. You will have to figure out how much sleep you actually need to operate at a peak level through trial and error. Some people's sleep schedules are random; they don't even know their ideal sleep hours.

What is your peak number? For me, six hours of sleep is needed for me to operate at my peak level. I can do well on five, but six is more ideal. You have to figure out what that number is for you as every person's body and sleep needs are different.

I'm emphasizing this bedtime routine because you cannot build up with one hand, tear down with the other, and hope to be successful. This means you can't have this fantastic morning routine and just go to bed really late consistently. If you repeatedly do this, you won't be giving yourself the rest you need to make your routine sustainable.

In Japanese war camps, sleep deprivation was the number one tactic used to gain information from captured prisoners. If you think about it this way, you realize that you're actually torturing yourself when you deprive yourself of sleep.

When I reflect on the Miracle Morning by Hal Elrod, it makes me think about these three nighttime reminders that I want to bring to your attention. The first nighttime reminder is the bedtime affirmations that I pulled directly out of this book. Here it is. Don't be alarmed by the times as they are just placeholders for whatever times you decide.

"I am going to bed tonight at 9:30 p.m. and waking up at 3:30 a.m., which gives me six hours of sleep. This is, in fact, exactly what I need in order to perform at a peak level tomorrow. The reality is my mind controls my body, and I really only need as much sleep as I tell myself and choose to believe that I need.

Many of the most successful people in history function optimally on four to six hours of sleep, and I cannot allow myself to fall into the limiting belief that I'll improve my life by sleeping more. In fact, it will soon be seriously detrimental to my stress level, finances, relationships, career, and lifestyle goals. My quality of life as I know it depends on my waking up on time tomorrow. "

Please do not feel any pressure to live on 4-6 hours of sleep, but just don't allow yourself to fall into a lie that you need more sleep than you actually do. The bedtime affirmations helped me remind myself of why I was going to bed at that time and then motivated me to wake up in the morning.

Nighttime reminder number two is to set your alarm. There's an app you can use on your phone, where you can just set your sleep time. However, regardless of what alarm you use, make sure you have the RIGHT time set before shutting your eyes.

Nighttime reminder number three is distancing your phone from you—put it across the room after setting your alarm while your phone is on do not disturb. This is great for having a clear mind, not scrolling through social media, or listening to a YouTube video for at least 15 minutes before sleep. This will prime your mind to wake up in peak state. If you're married, it's a good time to connect with your spouse instead of having a noisy head.

Other nighttime reminder honorable mentions are to set your clothes out for the next day. I like to do this with my exercise clothes to eliminate this decision in the morning. I also listen to something motivational during my evening grooming to give my mind a bath from whatever dirty limiting beliefs seek space in my mind from the day.

You may want to tweak your evening routine from the aforementioned recommendations, but stick to whatever you decide. Remember, a successful morning starts the night before. Find the bedtime affirmation worksheet at bit.ly/infocusbookresources.

Application

   2. Complete the Bedtime Affirmation Worksheet

CHAPTER 20

ESTABLISHING YOUR WORKFLOW ROUTINE

N ow that we've covered the morning and evening aspects of your day, we will now cover the very important middle of your day. Again, you may be thinking you need more time in your day. However, we often wish we had more time in a day because we waste half our time with unproductive distractions, not because we actually need more time. Seven deadly distractions that kill productivity in a workday are as follows:

1. Scrolling on social media
2. Phone conversations with family and friends
3. Office conversations with coworkers
4. Audio talk
5. Housework
6. Helping Others
7. TV

Scrolling on social media

Have you ever had the experience of getting on a social network platform such as Facebook or Instagram with one purpose, and all of a sudden, 30 minutes have passed, and you still haven't done what you came to the platform for? This has happened too many times for me to count. Social network platforms are designed to draw you in and keep you in for long periods. Deleting the apps off my phone has skyrocketed my productivity. A great documentary to check out for eye-opening revelations regarding social media is Social Dilemma on NetFlix.

Phone conversations and family and friends

Nothing throws off a productive day like a good family and friends' crisis. This person is upset with this person, and that person is struggling with that situation; the crises are endless when we answer the phone when we should be working. We must guard our working time blocks with all diligence. Otherwise, the time will come and go. Then, we will end the day feeling unproductive and stressed out.

Office conversations with coworkers

When on a plane, and in the case of an emergency, it is said to put your mask on first before you can help anyone else. This is a principle to remember whenever interacting and helping coworkers at work. We all want to be a resource to others, but we must put boundaries in place to make sure we are not extending ourselves so far that our work suffers, or even worse, we work way passed our paid time and infringe on our family time. Watch out for this one.

Audio Talk

Many people tend to listen to radio shows or podcasts while at work. The problem with this activity is that it occupies crucial brain space and causes you to use mind power to engage with the material and form opinions and thoughts that take away from deep work production. If you work a physical repetition job that doesn't require deep thinking, listening to personal & business development books can be advantageous. This is the one exception for this category.

Housework

For those who work from home, housework always calls your name. Whether it's folding clothes, doing the dishes, or doing other house chores, there's always something to do. If you're not working from home, it's even more crucial not to get caught up in housework when trying to build something because your time is even more limited.

Helping Others

While it is a blessing to give and help others, you must make sure you are covering your personal promises to yourself before helping others. You must not give away your rent or mortgage money to help someone; otherwise, you and your family won't have money to shelter yourselves. Somehow we view our finances this way, but not our time. However, time is the only asset that we cannot get back. Perhaps this is why I hate watching movies that are several hours long.

TV

The danger of Netflix and all other forms of viewing platforms is that it takes more energy to stop watching a show we enjoy than it does just to keep watching. We also lie to ourselves. We say we deserve a break. The truth is, we do not deserve to watch TV all day. Create restrictions on when you will watch TV as binge-watching is definitely an undefeated time waster.

The truth is, if it's anything other than the one thing that you're supposed to be doing at that moment, it's a distraction. Since these deadly distractions are very prominent weapons in blocking productivity, I want to offer this thought process. What is the lead domino in terms of eliminating all or most of these distractions in one sweep?

One thing that I've found to be the lead domino in eliminating distractions is your environment. If you're in the right place, certain distractions just don't exist. If you position yourself in the office where people aren't talking, this will no longer be a distraction. If you delete the social media apps off your phone, you don't scroll nearly as frequently. If you put your phone on do not disturb during work hours, family and friends can't call you when you are not open to talking. If you delete the podcasts you love to waste time on your phone, it makes it inconvenient to download them again; thus, you end up listening less. If you work from Starbucks, you can't stare at the unfolded laundry and be tempted to do things other than being productive on your one thing. Also, if you unplug your TV when you're not watching it, it provides enough of a barrier that might be just enough to deter you from watching it at the moment. That one second in a crucial decision could make all the difference in your productivity. Outside is a phenomenal place to work, as well. Your brain is open, and the sunlight provides natural energy and increases your ability to have a better sleep. The environment is key. What's your bunker? That's what I call it. Where do you go? Where is your number one productive spot?

Now that we've gone over the 7 deadly distractions and environment kryptonite for the distractions, I want to share my four workflow winners to implement for increased productivity as well.

Number one is an isolated environment. Pick an environment that is as isolated as possible because some of us work around people. It may not be totally possible to be in an isolated environment. When it's not that time where you need to be collaborating, and you need time for deep work, an isolated environment is invaluable.

Number two is place your phone on do not disturb. It won't kill you to put your phone on do not disturb for an hour or two in your productive work blocks. Those just checks and notifications that just pop up, again and again, will drive you crazy trying to complete any significant deep work. It's the reason why it's so hard for people to get things done efficiently and quickly.

The third workflow winner is to listen to study music while working. I rotate through a few different stations on Pandora that keep me locked in on my deep work. Those stations are beats for studying radio, instrumental hip hop radio, Christian hip hop radio, or film score radio.

The fourth workflow winner is limit email. My recommendation is to check emails only two times a day. I know it might sound crazy, but I deleted the email app off my phone, and it definitely improved my productivity. Restricting when you open email prevents you from being bogged down by other people's agenda every day, never truly accomplishing your own. The time you check should not be the first thing in the morning or when you start work. I want you to commit to your most important one thing first. You can delegate the email task to an assistant at some point, but for now, I recommend limiting your email interaction.

Often we wish we had more time in a day because we waste half of our time with unproductive distractions, not because we actually need more time. Implement these four things and review your weekly focus plan and stick to it. Remember, if it's not your one thing, it's a distraction. I can't repeat that statement enough. Anything that is not your one thing is a distraction.

Application:

Implement the 4 workflow winners:

1. Isolated Environment

2. Place Phone on Do Not Disturb During Deep Work Time Blocks
3. Listen to Study Music while Completing Deep Work
4. Limit Email Checks to Two Times a Day

CHAPTER 21

ESTABLISHING ACCOUNTABILITY

As you plan and prepare for your routines, an element
that is just as important is accountability.
"Accountability is the glue that ties the commitment
to the result." - Bob Proctor.
"What I've learned firsthand is the achievement
gap to reach your goals is association and
accountability." – Kendall Ficklin

Association is a larger body of people with a common
productive direction with undeniable momentum and
a clear vision. There's no way you can get a large
group of people to come together if there's no vision
of what drew them there. It has to be clear.

Accountability is an individual who will challenge you and
remind you of what you committed to from the common
association. For example, I'm apart of Breathe University,
made up of a group of people all moving in the same direction

with undeniable momentum and a clear vision. Within Breathe University, are a diverse group of experts in all areas of life from which I have accountability partners.

In grad school, I went to the gym consistently. There were people with me, and for whatever reason, it made going to the gym easier. However, when I was on my own, I could skip a workout, and no one knew. On the contrary, when I go to the gym with others, they know when I skip. There's just a different way that you operate when you have to answer to someone. However, no one will do this for you. You have to establish accountability for yourself.

Here's what you can do to bring this idea from theory to practice. Identify the three most important areas in your life. Indicate your association and accountability to ensure successful results in that area.

You can access the core value accountability worksheet at bit.ly/infocusbookresources. You'll find an example of my core value accountability structure. My three most important areas are faith, family, and finances. In the example, you can see my association and accountability.

For instance, for my faith, I have Liquid Church as my association. This association is growing and has a clear mission to saturate the state of New Jersey with the gospel of Jesus Christ. There are a lot of like-minded people who are galvanizing around that mission.

Within that association, I have accountability through my Campus Pastor. This person is more like mentor accountability for me. I also have another layer of accountability with another gentleman represented by the initials in my example. This person could be more of a peer/mentee type of person within the association. The bottom line is there is someone aware of your progress and commitments.

Accountability works best when you have a mentor, mentee, and peer directions all covered. Even a mentee helps to hold you accountable because how can you lead someone unless you're actually following through on the advice you're giving them? Therefore, I like to have a person that I'm holding accountable, or we're holding each other accountable. How can I teach them unless I'm doing it?

The other areas are laid out for you on the core value accountability resource. Remember, accountability is the glue that ties the commitment to the result. Don't ever forget that. I wouldn't have written this book or be having the success I'm experiencing in business if I didn't have it for all the different areas of my life where I seek success. Extraordinary success is not achieved alone. Be sure to follow through on establishing accountability for yourself.

Application

1. Complete the Core Value Accountability Worksheet

CHAPTER 22

EFFICIENT & RELEVANT INDUSTRY RESEARCH

ere's one thing I know about you. You don't know what you don't know. The great American philosopher Forrest Gump told us, "Life is like a box of chocolates, you never know what you're going to get." My addition to this quote is, "You buy some chocolate in life you wouldn't, if you knew the filling that was inside." You might be saying, what does this have to do with anything? Well, how it connects to industry research is we have no shortage of information out there. How do you get good information in a world full of information? Here's my number one industry research philosophy to keep you in the know.

It is google alerts. Let's talk about google alerts for a second. The significance of Google alerts is Google alerts actually takes the most relevant industry research, the most frequently clicked, highest-quality information, and sought after industry content in one email.

You no longer have to browse around the internet aimlessly researching your industry. All you need to do is follow the worksheet that you can access at bit.ly/infocusbookresources. First, you go to google.com/alerts and log into your Gmail account where you want to receive your alerts. Then, make sure your alert is set for every day because an entrepreneur is an everyday lifestyle. It's simply a powerful tool.

Simply follow along with that sheet, and your google alerts will be complete. Schedule at least 30 to review your google alerts daily. Just 30 minutes a day can make a significant dent in your industry research knowledge base.

I recommend that you not read or watch videos for the entire 30 minutes but take 15 minutes to listen to something or read something and the other 15 minutes to apply or create a plan for the information.

After completing the systematic industry research worksheet, schedule your learning time. What is the time you will commit to your research daily? This research provides a spark to help you stay sharp as an entrepreneur with content creation and development, along with your general knowledge and mastery of your subject matter. You will also come across top industry books and programs as you do your research, which you can also spend time researching. I am a huge audiobook consumer to speed up my learning curve. Previously, I only read about six books maximum for the year; now, I can consume multiple books a month. However, I want to further emphasize applying the information and not just consuming it.

Using this strategy, you will be sure to have a golden nugget for your audience when you lock into one subject and make it pop every day. When you consistently focus on one subject daily, you'll be that top-level expert that you seek to be in your industry in no time.

Application:

2. Complete the Systematic Industry Research Worksheet

CHAPTER 23

BUILDING A PERFORMANCE REVIEW SYSTEM

Dwelling on your past success is the greatest
enemy to your future success.

This is a lesson that a company like Blockbuster exemplifies most. They were synonymous with movies. People religiously said, "Make it a blockbuster night." We still call the big hit movies blockbusters. However, the company no longer exists. What a humbling thought to know that your former company's name is embedded in the language of American culture, but you do not exist.

Sadly, they could have certainly seen Netflix coming. Netflix looked to partner with blockbuster initially, but blockbuster rested on their laurels and didn't fully understand the trend they would start. They didn't see where the industry was going; therefore, they missed the boat. I would suggest they missed the boat because they didn't have a consistently open feedback loop where they were seeking to improve. They didn't have a strategic review system focused on trends and the way things were moving. They must've had a decent system to get as big as they got, but I don't know if it reached a point where they got comfortable. They sat on their hands, dwelled on their past success, and it was the enemy to their future success.

Your feedback loop may be monthly, weekly, or daily, depending on your industry and business activities. However, you need to have a feedback loop. Taking the approach of what got you here will keep you here is a surefire way to stunt growth and prevent long term success.

Please see the business evaluation tools at bit.ly/infocusbookresources. I have a bi-weekly staff meeting with my private business mastermind group. We partner to discuss the strengths, weaknesses, opportunities, and threats for our businesses. This evaluation tool is called the SWOT analysis.

This is a way you can lean into the strengths of your business. You can develop a plan to support your weaknesses. You can seize growth opportunities, and eliminate threats. Let me break this down further. Your strengths are what you know you do well and gives you the highest profitability of your business activities. You may be evaluating things such as where are you bringing in the most profit? How is the customer experience?

You have to know what you do well because when you sell people on your business, you need to communicate clearly what an individual is getting out of the experience of partnering with you regardless of your industry. Knowing your strengths is significant so that you keep pressing the gas pedal on what you do best. It's also significant in your marketing and what you share with others about your business.

The next thing is your weaknesses. There are things that, inevitably, you don't do well. There are advantages and disadvantages to any level of business. For instance, if you think about a small business, the customer experience could be phenomenal because if you have fewer clients you're dealing with, you could give them more attention.

That's why I was able to do more one on one coaching as my business was growing and I was smaller coaching and consulting company. In comparison, my weakness would probably be some of the power tools that I'm simply could not exercise as far as growing my business faster because of a lack of resources.

Conversely, a larger company might work like a machine but lack the small customer care advantage. However, wherever we fall on the spectrum, these weaknesses must be addressed. For example, if a business owner recognizes building an email list is their weakness, they could take a course on building an email list. They can hire a strong consultant in that area or a coach to help them level up.

The next thing is opportunities. These are not weaknesses, but things that can easily be used to advance the ball in your business. These are things you have the ability, expertise, and time to implement. One of the opportunities a business owner could see in adding extra value to their personal coaching experience is adding a group chat where more intimate conversation and accountability occur among clients.

It's one thing to go through coursework on your own, but it's another thing to be reminded where your focus should be by the group as you're going through it. What exists for you to drive your business forward even more?

Then, you look at the threats. This is the stuff that could take you out if you're not careful. If you don't fix this, you'll be out of business. Maybe this won't be tomorrow, but like Blockbuster, maybe down the road.

On the bottom part of the SWOT resource, you'll find spaces for three action items. What are the top three action items that come out of that evaluation session? Who is the person that's going to complete each of those action items? Who can you barter or partner with to follow up on any of these action items?

This is the main activity that I use, but I like to flip flop between SWOT and another activity to prevent things from getting stale. It's like muscle confusion. You want to keep yourself nimble and loose. The other review system I've learned from other business consultants is Stop, Start, and Continue.

The question goes, if you were starting your business today, knowing what I now know, what would you stop doing? What are the activities that are actually busy work? What activities aren't giving you the biggest bang for your buck? What should you stop?

The second question is, if you were starting your business today, knowing what you now know, what would you start doing? What should you be doing now that you weren't doing before? What has the potential to give you the biggest bang for our buck? What should you start?

The third question is, if you were starting your business today, what would you continue? What things in your business are already working for you and should roll forward? This question correlates to your strengths in the SWOT analysis. We get focused on changes, but there are inevitably some things that may be working in your business that you want to keep doing. This exercise is a different way of breaking down the information that may spark a different part of your brain than the SWOT analysis.

Through this review process, continue to ask yourself question after question. What if this? What if that? Why? Because questions start to create a new reality for what you're capable of. Remember, dwelling on your past success is the greatest enemy to your future success. Access both the SWOT Analysis and Stop, Start, and Continue activity at bit.ly/infocusbookresources

Keep in mind these activities are not one and done. They are ongoing. I recommend creating a folder or a system for this, where you keep these files and date them as you do them. You will certainly want to schedule a time to review. When are you doing this? Do you want to know what is making your business thrive? What is making your businesses die? When are you learning this?

This one activity will make a significant difference for you and ensure that your business never becomes BlockBuster.

Application

1. Download the SWOT Analysis worksheet and schedule time to do it regularly
2. Download the STOP, START, & CONTINUE worksheet and schedule time to do it regularly

CHAPTER 24

THE POWER OF COACHING

H ere's a philosophy we often get wrong. We say practice makes perfect. But one of the greatest coaches of all time, Vince Lombardi, who was responsible for the first couple of super bowl wins with the Green Bay Packers in American football history, said, "Practice doesn't make perfect, perfect practice makes perfect." When you think of going to the gym and doing pushups, you may feel you're doing them correctly. However, a health coach or personal trainer will let me know if you actually are. They will let you know if you need to raise your midsection, lower it, move your hands forward, back, wider, or closer for the greatest yielding results.

Often the biggest shortcut to massive success is finding a person to study. This is the greatest lesson that I learned from the life of Kobe Bryant. He literally studied Michael Jordan and simply did what he did with his own flair and flavor. That's what I'm encouraging you to do. Watch your person like a hawk.

Follow them on social media, join their online communities, join their coaching programs, volunteer at their events, examine how they do their work and details of their work closely.

Reach out to them with questions about specific areas you need help with, and ask for feedback on how they overcame a similar challenge in the past. You really want to establish no more than three main sources of information and use all other knowledge as a supporting compliment. In high school, I prepared my admissions essay and had a group of different teachers review it. By the fourth or fifth teacher, I was confused. Each had a different philosophy on how things should be done.

Therefore, my paper had a lack of focus. I probably should have gone to a guidance counselor who was reviewing college essays all the time and know what the colleges are looking for, or an admissions staff person would be even better. What I found in this experience was that each person had their point of emphasis that took away my paper's identity.

The point is I had a whole bunch of people telling me what to do, and I was more confused than when I started. That may be the truth about you. It's easy to fall into this trap because there's so much information out there. Lock into no more than three sources of business owners you would model your business after, and use all other information you come across as complimentary. However, I want you to give the information at least a year to work. There are no microwave tricks, even though many will try to convince you of this. I'm not saying you have to struggle the way others did when the information wasn't so easily accessible. But what I am saying is to achieve the extraordinary results you seek, it takes extraordinary focus, hard work, and dedication. As I like to say, you must be locked in.

This is the single principle I attribute most to my success in business. Here's how I did it. I found the person whose voice resonated with me the most. You may know someone who's voice resonates with you the most. When they speak, you feel they are speaking your language. They also sound like they understand the language you speak.

Interestingly enough, the person that I decided to follow is from my home state. They had a rhythm to their language, how they operated, and how they moved that resonated with me. I didn't even know that initially, but once that came out, I said that makes sense. I thought to myself, it's no coincidence I understand what they are saying so clearly.

I joined their coaching community, and I simply modeled my business after their business and enhanced it with my own flavor. I wouldn't suggest you pick me as your coach unless the language I speak resonates with you. However, I suggest you get a coach/model if you do not want a lid on your results. If you don't want a lid on your results, a coach is absolutely necessary, as most of us need some type of system to follow to build momentum and practice perfectly. Let me say this because you may be disagreeing in your mind. You may think that I can figure this out on my own, but I'll stick with the basketball reference.

As great as all-time great basketball player Michael Jordan was, he had no championship success without Phil Jackson. And guess what? Neither did Kobe Bryant. As a matter of fact, it's been suggested that we look at Kobe's career in two separate ways—Kobe with Phil and Kobe without Phil. It's like being in a batting cage, and you're making certain adjustments that you can feel you need to make, but you're still not hitting the ball well. However, the coach who stands outside the cage looking in can tell you. "Hey, you need to bring your right foot back a little bit. You need to bring your elbow up." They just have a different perspective that helps you accelerate your advancement. Please hear me out. Out of all the entrepreneurship principles I've shared in this book, this one will moved the needle more than any others.

If I become your coach, I'm looking forward to making you focused and better!

However, do me a favor. If I ever go away or stop getting better for any reason, find another coach. Results should be your top priority. Remember, what one of the greatest coaches of all time told us, "Practice doesn't make perfect. Perfect practice makes perfect." – Vince Lombardi

So stop scurrying around, randomly and aimlessly. Extraordinary results come from being INFOCUS. Identify who you will begin to study. Study them. Then, keep studying them. Most importantly, implement what you learn. There's no point in studying a person if you never make a move.

One of the most significant studies I implemented was being in a community that had a daily call on entrepreneurship.

Then, I implemented the same type of daily call with my own flavor. That call quickly grew to dozens of people because of the impact.

I would have never thought of this game-changing idea simply doing research online, as this idea was not found in any of my research. Here are the 5 things that are in it for you when you hire a coach.

1. Accelerates your progress and creates successes because they've done it before for themselves and other clients
2. Has an arsenal of techniques and an understanding of business building
3. Provides access to additional vetted resources to help support your business
4. Creates more meaningful discussion with options and objective opinions, that gives their client flexibility
5. And provides patient support and accountability so you don't feel like you are in this by yourself.

If you are interested in working with me, schedule a 30-minute discovery call at bit.ly/30minchatchew. I'm confident that what you learned here will keep you growing and unstuck. I hope you now have the blueprint to stop side hustling and make one business pop! I can't wait to hear your results!

Application

1. Book a free consultation with me at bit.ly/rp30minchatchew

ABOUT THE AUTHOR

After walking away from my career of 7+ years as a student affairs professional, I launched my consulting business because I wanted more income, more freedom, and more impact on the world.

Since transforming from student affairs professional to work from anywhere business consultant, I've worked with dozens of motivated entrepreneurs to identify their unique advantages in the marketplace and create a plan for increased productivity & business success.

With a knack for asking the right questions, real life training & experience as a serial entrepreneur, and a hard earned MBA, I'm equipped to help you overcome the roadblocks that are in the way of you running a profitable business.

Armed with a proven methodology, a safe & welcoming coaching style, and a genuine desire to see you win, I'm here for you!

Let me help you stop side hustling & make one business pop!

Book a free consultation with me at bit.ly/rp30minchatchew

www.ingramcontent.com/pod-product-compliance
Lightning Source LLC
Chambersburg PA
CBHW062124040426
42337CB00044B/3973